"I've devoted my career to inspiring entrepreneurs to build the business of their dreams. That begins with people—hiring, developing, and keeping the best. Jeff's book lays out step-by-step how to do it. Don't think about starting or running a company without Recruit Rockstars."

—JOHN LEE DUMAS, FOUNDER, ENTREPRENEURS ON FIRE

"Smart leaders listen to Jeff. When it comes to recruiting, he's a whiz. This is the insider's guide!"

—DAVID COHEN, FOUNDER AND CO-CEO, TECHSTARS

"Leading remarkable people to fulfill an important mission is what business is all about. And that starts with recruiting only the best. Jeff has devoted his career to this art, and reveals exactly how to do it."

—SYDNEY FINKELSTEIN, PROFESSOR OF LEADERSHIP, DARTMOUTH COLLEGE, AND BESTSELLING AUTHOR OF SUPERBOSSES

"Jeff outlines in practical and compelling terms why hiring Rockstar talent is more critical than ever. He also provides a clear framework for applying both art and science to help leaders create a Rockstar culture."

—STEVE MILOVICH, FORMER SVP GLOBAL HUMAN RESOURCES, DISNEY/ABC TELEVISION

"Jeff has mined his unusually broad and deep experience as a leader, recruiter, teacher, and student of talent to provide original and impactful ways organizations can create winning cultures. In a time of disruption and unpredictability, building a team of Rockstars is the surest way to not just survive, but excel."

—CHRISTIE HEFNER, FORMER CHAIRMAN AND CEO, PLAYBOY ENTERPRISES

"A company is the sum total of its people. Building a Best Place to Work requires hiring top performers who embrace our culture. I wish I had this book along the way! I have long admired Jeff, and I appreciate his priceless wisdom to finding and landing the best."
— GEORGE H. WALKER, CHAIRMAN AND CEO, NEUBERGER BERMAN

"Jeff recruited two amazing SVPs for us in half the time of the big recruiting firms. He brought such outstanding candidates to the table, it was a very difficult decision. Jeff's a trusted advisor, with an insanely high standard of talent."
— ALEX STEPIEN, CEO, CAPPEX

"I'd been absorbing Jeff's articles and podcasts for years and became frustrated that my own sales leaders weren't delivering on his prescriptions. When it came time to look for a new Chief Revenue Officer, I turned to Jeff and asked him to find us a Rockstar. He did a deep dive into our company's expectations and culture and attacked the search. I didn't think it was possible, but Jeff managed to deliver four high-quality leaders for in-person interviews (including the Rockstar we ultimately hired) within thirty days. Today, I've gone from frustrated to excited again about delivering on our sales potential, largely due to Jeff's efforts."
— ROB GLANDER, PRESIDENT AND CEO, GWC WARRANTY

"A recruiting vet shows why Rockstars are the key to building corporate value and offers step-by-step advice on how to attract them and keep them challenged."
— PATRICK KENEALY, MANAGING DIRECTOR, RIDGE VENTURES

"As a sixth-generation family business with 2,500 professionals, attracting, engaging, and empowering top talent is our highest priority—they do the rest. Jeff's step-by-step guide informs and reinforces our approach to people and many of the principles that have made us a top workplace. Recruit Rockstars is a key read for every current and aspiring leader who believes people are the answer."

—JENNIFER ALTER WARDEN, COO, BAIRD & WARNER

"If you read one book this year to grow your company, this is it. Building and keeping a team of high-impact players is the leader's first job. Recruit Rockstars reveals how it's done."

—DAYTON OGDEN, HEAD OF TALENT AND RECRUITING, SUMMIT PARTNERS

"Building a world-class business requires attracting and retaining world-class talent. This has become an increasingly critical success factor, as companies today must adapt to rapidly changing market forces and emerging technologies. This guide is without peer in revealing how a top executive recruiter secures the best talent for organizations. Now, you can do the same!"

—BRUCE CAZENAVE, CEO, NAUTLIUS

RECRUIT ROCKSTARS

RECRUIT ROCKSTARS

THE 10 STEP PLAYBOOK TO FIND THE WINNERS AND IGNITE YOUR BUSINESS

JEFF HYMAN

LIONCREST
PUBLISHING

RECRUIT ROCKSTARS

The 10 Step Playbook to Find the Winners and Ignite Your Business

ISBN   978-1-61961-815-2 *Hardcover*

978-1-61961-817-6 *Paperback*

978-1-61961-816-9 *Ebook*

DEDICATED TO MY ROCKSTARS
JONAH, MAXWELL, DEANN

CONTENTS

IIIIIIIIIIIIIIIIIIIIII

LET'S TAKE THE GUESSWORK OUT OF RECRUITING

||||||||||||||||||||

Not so long ago, baseball talent scouts relied on instincts, experience, and intuition. A scout, often a former ballplayer, trusted his gut. Then, along came a new breed of scout: young, Ivy League-educated math whizzes who might not have held a bat since Little League. This new generation grew skeptical of the hit-and-miss results of eyeballing prospects, and instead put their faith in statistical probabilities and the burgeoning field of sabermetrics, as illustrated in Michael Lewis' book, which was later made into the hit film, *Moneyball*.

It's easy to scoff at the criteria the older generation of scouts relied on: tea leaves such as, "Does the prospect have a confident walk?" and "How pretty is his girlfriend?" and other wildly irrelevant indicators of on-field performance. However, before you pick up stones to throw, consider the way in which you hire your company's talent. Are you relying on your personal experience and instincts or have you installed a sabermetrics-like system designed to minimize the risk of drafting a bust?

A baseball team is only as good as the players who comprise it. Identifying the best available players at each position should, therefore, be the most critical function of every team. The same is true in any profession. I realize that I'm biased, but as a fact and not just an opinion, recruiting great people is without a doubt the most important thing in business.

Don't just take my word for it. According to the 2016 Conference Board CEO Challenge Survey, attracting and retaining talent is the number one concern of CEOs, regardless of their company size or industry. That wasn't always the case. Up until very recently, finding customers was the top-priority issue, but now that we've hit record-low unemployment, talent is at a premium. Thus, the biggest impediment to growth is the scarcity of talent, particularly "Rockstars," in the labor market.

Noam Wasserman, Professor of Clinical Entrepreneurship at the University of Southern California, estimates that 65 percent of growth companies fail due to people problems.

That's due to either the wrong hires, people in the wrong roles, a lousy culture, or poor relationships between colleagues. If people are the driving force behind your team's success, then by that same token, people are likely the driving force behind your team's lack of success.

If you use science—and not your gut—and make the effort to recruit the best people, your company's potential is limitless. It will win its market and continue to attract and retain A-Players, or what I call Rockstars. This book is the manual for recruiting Rockstars. As such, it could be the most important business book you ever read.

Here's the scary statistic: The national batting average of hires who meet or beat the hiring manager's expectations two years after being hired is .500. In other words, 50 percent. That's right...no more accurate than the flip of a coin. Half of new hires work out, and half fall short. Nevertheless, nearly every business executive I've encountered believes deep down that they're strong at assessing talent. They trust their gut. That institutionalized hubris is the primary reason there is little discussion on this subject. Yet, that 50 percent failure rate would be unacceptable in any other aspect of business, particularly when the cost of fixing the problem is so minimal.

By employing the methodology within these pages, I guarantee that you will increase your hiring success rate to 80 percent, 90 percent, or more. It'll never be 100 percent—no recruiting process is flawless. But this isn't rocket science. Recruiting is like any other business skill you hope to master, whether it's strategy, marketing, or raising capital. It requires focus, committing to an objective, and a standardized process that relies on things that are actually predictive of success.

This 10-step process is based on the patterns that I've observed in recruiting more than 3,000 people in my twenty-five years as a startup founder, a CEO, and an executive recruiter. I've over-hired and under-hired; I've overpaid and underpaid; I've had people quit the first day on the job. I've made every mistake in the book, and along the way, I've learned how to de-risk hiring. I decided to write this book because I want to help you avoid the mistakes that I've made, accelerate the growth of your business, reduce the number of people you must fire, and find more enjoyment—not only in your business life but also in your personal life.

There are surprisingly few books about recruiting, and the few that do exist are nuts-and-bolts guides that provide how-to instructions for HR managers. Buried in the bookstore shelves of tomes on marketing, selling, raising capital, leadership, and the like, you'll find just a handful of dust-covered books on recruiting talent. The great irony is that the most important aspect of a business is treated so haphazardly that a coin toss would yield equally accurate results. I don't understand business leaders who don't obsess over it and feel compelled to improve.

90 PERCENT OF BUSINESS PROBLEMS ARE ACTUALLY RECRUITING PROBLEMS IN DISGUISE.

One mistake that nearly all companies make is simply one of nomenclature. They view recruitment as a "cost" rather than an "investment." The return on investment in people is exponentially greater than the return on any other resource, whether it's advertising, research and development, or acquisitions of other companies to provide growth. Note, too, that those expenditures are rightfully termed "investments" to be made as opposed to "costs" to be minimized.

Conversely, the cost of mis-hiring is staggering, both in terms of hard and soft costs. Countless studies peg the cost of a bad hire at three times the annual compensation of that particular employee. This includes the hard costs (recruiting, training, onboarding, severance, termination costs) and the soft costs (time spent micromanaging, employee morale from carrying the C-Player, damaged customer relationships, mistakes, missed business opportunity, disruption, and lost institutional knowledge). That's right—the $100K sales rep you just canned cost your company over $300K.

Yet, the revolving door turns ever faster at most companies. Per a recent survey by Leadership IQ, 46 percent of new hires are no longer with the company after eighteen months, and only 19 percent of new hires could be declared by the hiring manager as an unequivocal success. Only 19 percent.

If you think this problem is limited to lower-level employees, it isn't: Four out of ten CEOs fail during their first eighteen months, according to the Center for Creative Leadership. In fact, a *Harvard Business Review* study puts the failure rate among management hires at up to 60 percent, while pointing out that, in 80 percent of these cases, employee turnover was the result of faulty hiring.

Not only does turnover generate recurring hiring and firing costs, it disrupts continuity, erases institutional knowledge, and worst of all, wreaks all this havoc *unnecessarily*.

TALENT AS COMPETITIVE DIFFERENTIATOR

I've come to believe that the only true sustainable competitive differentiator in the business world today is talent. This wasn't always the case, but something has fundamentally changed in recent years. There was a time when a company could create and defend a competitive moat with its technology, intellectual property, and patents. That's become incredibly difficult to maintain, as technology now can be easily replicated, patents can be circumvented, and the cost of litigation to defend IP can be bankrupting for all but the largest of companies. Unless you have a war chest, forget about relying on IP to keep your competitors at bay. Additionally, consumer demand for transparency and technology sharing has expanded the realm of public domain.

Technology, being unsustainable, is no longer the barrier it once was.

Brand-building was the other formerly viable means of competitive differentiation. Thirty years ago, the nation watched three television networks each evening. Advertise, and voilà!—your brand was born. That, too, has changed in the age of the Internet. The fragmentation of media has led to a consumer diaspora. Building a brand with customers first requires locating them, then messaging them uniquely in their micro-habitats. Furthermore, people have become skeptical of brands, particularly if those brands don't reflect their own values or fail to live up to their social obligations.

Building a brand is more difficult than ever and can take a decade or longer. Chances are, if you think you have meaningful brand awareness, you're drinking your own Kool-Aid.

On the other hand, building a culture that is aggressive, focused, creative, and innovative is a renewable competitive differentiation strategy. Every business in every industry should consider itself an "execution play," and will fail to execute without attracting and keeping the best.

In my work with countless employers, I've observed that only a handful have developed a Rockstar culture, an environment that attracts Rockstars and allows them to flourish, while promptly weeding out non-Rockstars. That is only because the leaders of these firms take talent seriously. Their companies pump out a steady stream of innovative and profitable products, wrapped in services that show customers the love. If you're tired of chasing your competitors, or struggling to stay one step ahead, it's time to make talent your differentiation strategy.

There's an adage that A-Players recruit A-Players, but B-Players recruit C-Players. Culture creation has incredible staying power, because Rockstars attract other Rockstars. It's a self-perpetuating cycle that tightens and strengthens a culture. With each additional Rockstar you add to your bench, you can actually feel your competitive moat deepening.

To be clear, I'm not suggesting merely upgrading your HR department. I'm proposing that the renewable resource of *talent* become your company's primary engine of competitive differentiation. If you build a culture that is so compelling that it lures Rockstars, you'll win. It's as simple as that. However, while it may be simple, it's not easy. But don't worry... that's where this book comes in.

In these pages, I'll show you step-by-step how to win the war for talent. And make no mistake, we're in nothing but an all-out war. Unemployment is near a record low. As of the writing of this book, it's about 4.2 percent. And among college-educated workers, that number is about 2 percent. This means that you must work tirelessly to build a compelling culture, pay competitively, and battle for the best talent. In other words, we are in a Rockstar's market. Every day, the nation's 90,000 headhunters like me are attempting to poach your best people.

If you commit to the principles in this book, you'll reduce your reliance on headhunters while simultaneously headhunter-proofing your company. By the way, despite the undisputed success of sabermetrics over the last few decades, by any measurement—all-star selections, winning percentage increase, World Series championships—the overwhelming majority of baseball teams still rely on the old, "I'll know it when I see it" philosophy.

WHY I WROTE THIS BOOK

I've started four businesses, three of which were recruiting companies. In total, between my own employees and the people that we've placed for our clients, I've recruited or hired over 3,000 people. I've raised more than $55 million of venture capital to fund those companies. I studied at Wharton as an undergraduate and received my MBA degree from Kellogg. I now teach the first course on recruiting that Kellogg has ever offered. I host a highly rated podcast, with interviews of hundreds of talent experts. I've spoken at countless recruiting conferences and been featured on CNBC, as well as in the *Wall Street Journal*, *Fortune*, *Forbes*, among a laundry list of publications. Recruiting has been my professional life for twenty-five years.

All that said, my most important qualification is none of those things. Instead, it's one that requires no education, formal training, or years of professional experience. I'm fanatical about recruiting and the impact it makes on the enterprise. You might say that I'm obsessive about it. That's why I created this 10-step playbook, which is the culmination of the wisdom I've gleaned as a student of this discipline.

The importance of talent to an organization remains misunderstood, and I'm on a mission to clarify it. In fact, I've made my personal mantra "No bad hires." One of the biggest mistakes that managers make is to treat people like commodities. I understand that growth companies are intensely focused on finding and keeping customers, but if you behave as if employees are interchangeable widgets, you've lost the game before you even take the field.

You can either spend time on the front end, carefully finding and recruiting Rockstars, or you can spend it on the back end in the form of micromanagement, inefficiencies, and ultimately, firings, in a cycle that keeps repeating itself until your haphazard process serendipitously lands a keeper.

I tell my clients and teach my MBA students that getting talent right in your company demands spending 30 to 50 percent of your time on recruiting and retention. It sounds impossible on its face, but a Rockstars-only company is so streamlined, self-regulating, and efficient that there is simply more time in a day. You can delegate with confidence, because Rockstars crave empowerment. They love a challenge and need not be micromanaged. You'll be more likely to meet your launch dates, hit your quarterly targets, and satisfy your Board and investors. You'll also have more time in your personal life—whether it's to take a vacation, spend time with family, or simply sleep with both eyes shut. It almost goes without saying that, ironically, you'll ultimately spend less time recruiting.

But as with everything in business, the fish stinks from the head down. If your company's CEO and Board of Directors aren't fully committed to assembling a team of Rockstars, the organization doesn't have a prayer of doing so. Providing a fair day's pay for a fair day's work is no longer sufficient. Millennials want more than money; they demand a compelling mission. They need to be inspired, which means—now more than ever—you must create such a strong culture that they wouldn't consider taking my phone call.

However, I should tell you that the executive search business is booming.

A 2016 LinkedIn study showed that 90 percent of all global

professionals are open to a new job opportunity. The irony is, despite the unemployment rate being at a record low, the level of dissatisfaction is at a record high. Most people hate their job, hate their boss, or are unengaged with their company or their role in it.

The good news is there are Rockstars out there willing to consider a career change. The bad news is that *your* Rockstars are among them.

What most hiring managers do (50% accuracy)		What hiring managers must do (90% accuracy)
Know what they want when they see it	**1**	All 4 interviewers agree upfront on the **Scorecard**
Focus on candidate's employers, titles, education	**2**	Focus on candidate's **DNA**, which determines behavior & performance
Boring & restrictive job description fails to attract candidates	**3**	Engaging **Job Invitation** compels Rockstars to have a confidential conversation
"Post & pray" with online job postings	**4**	Tap into personal **Network**, employees' networks, and LinkedIn Advanced Search
Waste time with unstructured interview questions	**5**	**Predict** success using structured interview questions
Rely solely on interviews to make the decision	**6**	Take final two candidates for a **Test Drive**
Call the provided references, after already making a decision	**7**	Reference the right way before making a decision, particularly **Backdoor References**
HR e-mails an uninspiring template offer letter	**8**	Hiring manager makes a strong verbal offer with **No Surprises**
Dump the new-hire into the pool. Good luck!	**9**	Get the first 30 days right with an **Onboarding Plan**. Remove **mis-hires** by day 60
Treat Rockstars the same as everyone else	**10**	**Differentiate** using challenge, candid coaching, and upside compensation to get the most out of Rockstars

PART I

PREPARE FOR ROCKSTARS

CHAPTER 1

KNOW WHAT YOU NEED

||||||||||||||||||

One of my clients, the CEO of a SaaS company, raised $15 million in venture capital in 2015. He came to me because he was missing his sales forecasts, as a result of his products being consistently late. He blamed the market, his competition, even his customers—everything but himself. After assessing his situation, I knew that I needed to get him to look in the mirror and admit he had a problem. The problem was people-related: vacancies, retention, and culture. For every issue that he could identify, I could tie it back to people.

It took some doing, but over the course of six months, we changed nearly everything about the way he ran the "people part" of his business. The playbook you're holding served as our guide. We determined what he needed his company's DNA to be built around, which meant removing mis-hires and low performers, reassigning people to the right roles, and establishing a leadership cadence. Most importantly, he committed to never settling for a B-Player again.

In less than two years, he is finally on a rapid path to profitability, and his Board couldn't be happier with his performance, particularly with regard to the quality of his new hires. His revenues are tripling year over year and it was only possible because he made building a Rockstar team his first priority. The key to turning around his business was to turn around how he hired.

MISCONCEPTIONS ABOUT ROCKSTARS

I've used this term quite a bit now without providing a definition. Hiring managers use their own definitions, but they're often soft and squishy—how many times have you heard "I really like him" or "She's a keeper"? Let's be specific. In my world, Rockstars are those in the top 5 percent of performers at the compensation level that we can afford, across two dimensions: competencies and DNA. You'll hear them referred to as A-Players, difference makers, gamechangers, or top performers. But there's so much fuzziness in all these labels that I need to be precise in what we're trying to identify. After all, if our ultimate goal is to remove subjectivity from recruiting, how can we even begin when we can't agree on what we're seeking?

For some, there is a negative connotation of the term, similar to "diva" or "prima donna," but that's not what I mean by Rockstar. We're only concerned with its positive connotations. Rockstar is shorthand for the best talent you can get your hands on to ensure that your company thrives.

An important note: I'm by no means implying that only 5 percent of people are hirable or worthy of successful careers. The other 95 percent just aren't a fit with your particular role and/or environment. They can very likely succeed in another company. Just as in romance, there's a lid for every pot. They either haven't discovered their gift or found the home to do their best work.

Somehow, a myth was born years ago that only certain key seats need to be filled by Rockstars and that the supporting cast should or can be B-Players, or that there's a bell curve model that makes for an ideal harmony. I want to dispel that dangerous notion. Think about a football team that invests a king's ransom in a franchise quarterback, then strings together a rag-tag offensive line as an afterthought. What good is it to have a Pro Bowl quarterback if you're not willing to keep him upright? He's not going to do much good on the disabled list.

LET'S PUT A ROCKSTAR IN EVERY SEAT.

As I write this, elite pro basketball players garner record-breaking salaries to play alongside other superstars. NBA teams have realized that winning championships requires acquiring top-notch talent in every position. Consider that Michael Jordan won a number of scoring titles but didn't win a single championship until the Bulls assembled star role players around him: Dennis Rodman, Steve Kerr, Scottie Pippen, Bill Cartwright, Horace Grant, Toni Kukoc, and B.J. Armstrong, among others who excelled at their individual roles. (I'm a Chicagoan...can you tell?)

For another thing, as the adage goes, it only takes one bad apple to spoil the bunch. A culture is an atmosphere created by the collective DNA of the individuals. Therefore, everyone in it is contributing to that culture—or detracts from it.

Then, there's the reality that Rockstars want to work with other Rockstars. You create synergies by assembling Rockstars. If you can't attract them at every position, maybe your company's mission isn't very compelling. Or maybe it's the leadership you're providing...or failing to provide.

THE TRUTH ABOUT ROCKSTARS

If the role is important enough to exist, it's important enough to have a Rockstar fill it. Yes, Rockstars will cost 20 percent more but can be two to three to ten times more effective than an average performer. Because of that effectiveness, you won't need to hire as many. I have a saying when it comes to Rockstars: "Recruit five, get the results of ten, and pay them like eight." Considered this way, they're actually a great value and simply the best investment you can make for your business.

If you take away nothing else from this book, I implore you to commit to never knowingly hiring a non-Rockstar again. When you hire Rockstars, the rest of your work largely takes care of itself.

That said, be careful, because a Rockstar at one company isn't necessarily one at another.

Rockstars are Rockstars because they are a fit in terms of both competencies and DNA characteristics. You can't simply make a play for a competitor's top sales rep and think she's going to produce equally well in your company. That's lazy recruiting.

Yet, this is exactly what happens during free agency in professional football. A player has performed at a Rockstar level with the team that drafted him, and when his contract is up, he offers his services to the highest bidder on the market. Another team will invariably overpay to fill a position of need, trusting that they're getting a proven commodity. High-priced free agents are anything but risk-free, however. Think about it: You're playing in a new city, for a new coach, in a new system, with a new playbook, new teammates, higher expectations, and more scrutiny. In business, it's the same thing: That other company is different than yours—

different culture, different values, different brand, different sales process, different funding, different *everything*. Don't presume that your competitor has made the same commitment to hiring Rockstars—they've got plenty of B-Players, and simply by "stealing" your competitor's trophy people, you may be unpleasantly surprised.

There's another problem in assuming Rockstar status translates from company to company: If the person you're targeting *truly* is a Rockstar, why would their employer ever let them get away? Franchise quarterbacks don't ever hit the free agent market, because the team offers them highly lucrative extensions at least a year before they finish playing out their current contract. You might well be poaching a B-Player from your competitor, doing them a favor while tarnishing your own culture, which does them yet another favor.

Perhaps you're hiring a competitor's sales rep. You might presume that you're not simply getting that person, what you're really getting is their stable of customers. The idea here is that those customers will be loyal to that salesperson and follow her from place to place. Unfortunately, the reality is those customers are loyal—to the company's products and services—not to the salesperson. Think about the scene from *Jerry Maguire* in which Jerry's been fired and is working the phones, scrambling desperately to take his clients with him. He ultimately keeps only one out of dozens, and it's the most unmanageable, demanding, labor-intensive client in the bunch. In my experience, hiring for someone's Rolodex is an awful idea.

Another assumption is that Rockstars can be developed. Sadly, C-Players never become B-Players, and B-Players rarely become A-Players. However, there are would-be Rockstars who are just in the wrong place. If you put them in the right spot, they'll shine. That's certainly true, but it's a mistake to think that you can create Rockstars out of just anyone. That's the rare exception.

It's also important to realize that Rockstars sometimes lose their Rockstar status. Just as music Rockstars fade from the charts or lose their sound, business Rockstars can also diminish over time. So it's important to review your talent on a regular basis.

It's lazy to simply hand-off hiring to the HR department. Your HR leader should be a valued consigliere, but if you want to de-risk your hiring, you must make every manager—regardless of functional responsibility—own their hiring process and results.

PUTTING A PRICE TAG ON ROCKSTARS

Before recruiting, it's vital to know up front precisely what you want and what are your non-negotiables. That is your bar, and you can't settle for less. By the end of this book, I hope you hear my voice in your head—reminding you that every time you settle, you're about to create a ton of extra work for yourself.

Bear in mind that there is no perfect candidate. You're not even looking for the best candidate. Theoretically, you might filter out the best candidate during the recruiting process. You're not seeking the perfect candidate; you're looking for the *safest* candidate. The one who is most likely to succeed in the role you seek to fill. The goal is to remove as much risk as is feasible, and in doing so, give yourself the highest probability of landing a Rockstar.

Knowing what you want includes knowing what you want to pay. This seems obvious, but that doesn't mean everyone adheres to it. If you don't have a clear budget in place, you're likely going to interview someone and fall in love, only to have your heart broken when you realize you can't afford that person.

One strategy, and I use the term loosely, is to interview a lot of candidates and develop a sense of what the going rate ought to be. The problem is that you might be letting Rockstars slip away while you're still calibrating the market. Interviewing a candidate that you don't intend to hire is a huge waste of your time.

In determining your budget, bear in mind the cost of a mis-hire discussed earlier. A recent survey by CareerBuilder points out that two-thirds of companies report that a bad hire costs them at least $25,000. Why not just pay a Rockstar candidate that money in the first place and avoid many of the hassles? Start with the high end of your budgeted range, and recruit a Rockstar, instead of trying to be cheap by hoping to hit the low end of your range.

In determining a budget, a site like Salary.com may be helpful as a starting point, but it's important to regularly benchmark compensation with other companies of similar size in the same city. I've found that compensation levels have become far more transparent because of the Internet and, thus, a lot more consistent. Three data points obtained from your local colleagues will usually suffice.

CREATE THE SCORECARD

The Scorecard is the yardstick by which all candidates will be measured. Since we're only interested in hiring Rockstars, this document reflects the gold standard. Let's be clear, a Scorecard is not a job description—"must have ten years of managerial experience, bachelor's degree from accredited college, knowledge of Excel, etc."—and isn't about a laundry list of requirements. On the contrary, the Scorecard is more of a standardized candidate grading system that identifies the tangible markers of success.

Everyone in the recruiting process—including the CEO, the Board, the investors—must consider it a sacred text. It may take some time to get everyone's input in quantifying the qualities you're looking to hire. That's fine; this process shouldn't be rushed. I simply do not commence a search for candidates, let alone interview, until everyone who will provide input into the process has agreed on the Scorecard. Invariably, there are differences of opinion as to what is necessary for the role—and this crucial phase forces those to be ferreted out and reconciled.

Scoring is based on a 1–10 rating system, with 9 and 10 being Rockstar level. A score of 7 or 8 has Rockstar potential and deserves consideration. Any candidate with a score below 7 should be eliminated from the process. That person isn't and most likely won't become a Rockstar in the given role. While you can entertain 7s, you should be looking to hire 8s and above at every position measured across two dimensions: role fit and company fit. 10s are virtually impossible to find—the black swan—so I focus on 8s and 9s. Imagine the possibilities for your company if every employee met this standard.

Role fit is based on the candidate's competencies for the job. Company fit is based on the degree to which their personal DNA matches the DNA of your company. I'll get to this in the next chapter.

Step 1 in creating the Scorecard is to envision what success looks like. Looking back eighteen months post-hire, what would need to be accomplished in order for the hiring manager to determine that they would enthusiastically re-hire the person? Write down what the benchmarks of success are—launching five new products, closing $1.5 million of new business, putting the company in the black, turning around the division, etc. Be specific and quantify wherever possible.

Step 2 is to define the day-to-day accountabilities—typically five to seven. Determine what the individual would need to do in order to deliver the degree of success identified in Step 1. What will this person actually be doing every day? It sounds silly, but many executives oversimplify this step—they don't connect the actual day-to-day tasks to the outcomes needed.

Step 3 is to define the competencies—think of these as characteristics—required to successfully execute those daily accountabilities. If one accountability, for instance, is to turn around an unprofitable product line, then the ability to ask insightful questions and prioritize problems to be solved might be an example of a necessary skill, as this person will need to uncover all the issues before crafting a solution. So, you might identify that competency as "intellectual curiosity."

In creating the Scorecard, it's vital to consider the specific point in the company's lifecycle. The Scorecard for the third software engineer in a startup phase, for example, looks far different from the fiftieth software engineer in a maturity phase. A CFO during growth phase is different from a CFO in a turnaround phase. You must be cognizant of every role at each stage: If you're in the startup phase, you want someone in the seat who's scrappy and innovative; if you're in a maturity phase, they need to be driven by value improvement, and so on. Relatively few employees who got you here will be well equipped to get you there. This is one of your hardest tasks, to continually upgrade your employee base to meet the challenges of your next phase.

Finally, Step 4 is to determine the candidate's DNA. Generally, the requisite DNA will not vary from position to position within your company, but it's as important to assess as competencies during the hiring process.

SO, WHAT IS DNA?

Even more than competencies, DNA is the most predictive element of success. It doesn't matter how competent a person is if their DNA doesn't match your company's ingrained DNA.

I'm not a believer in interviewing for "culture fit." Heresy, I know. Over the course of 10,000 candidate interviews, I've concluded that seeking a culture fit is just too fuzzy. I have yet to find a reliable data-driven way to do so. Instead,

I assess candidates in order to identify their personal DNA. By DNA, I'm referring to attributes that are hardwired at an early age and which rarely change over time, akin to genetic DNA. By the time we're eight years old, we are largely the person that we're going to be: detail-oriented, competitive, analytical, creative, etc. Those qualities will tell you much more about how a person will perform than last year's sales figures. Obviously, determining someone's DNA requires a great deal of digging, and that's why a lot of companies don't go through the effort. They might as well flip a coin.

There are reliable ways to identify DNA, and we'll look at them in the next chapter. In the meantime, if you'd like to download a free sample of the Scorecard, just go to www. RecruitRockstars.com/Bonus

THE CARDINAL SINS OF RECRUITING

Because I've seen my clients commit them over and over, I'd like to let you in on the most common offenses. No names mentioned.

LACK OF PROCESS

If you don't have a standardized recruiting system in place, whether it's mine or any other one, you might as well save yourself the time and draw a name out of a hat. If you aren't consistent in the way you evaluate candidates—if you ask different questions in each interview, for example—how can you possibly expect to compare and contrast among candidates?

UNCLEAR DNA

How can you hire people who share your company's DNA if you don't know what it is in the first place? At the risk of sounding alarmist, consider a hiring freeze until you resolve this issue. We'll discuss DNA extensively in the next chapter.

"POST AND PRAY"

Job boards have never been ideal but are notoriously troublesome during periods of low unemployment because few candidates are actively looking. You'll get hundreds of responses because it's become so easy for applicants to simply click "Apply." The next thing you know, your inbox is full. It's a way to feel like you're doing something, but it's a lazy, inefficient strategy that relies on hope.

RELY ON FACTORS NOT PREDICTIVE OF SUCCESS

Despite scientific evidence that these factors have little to no significant ability to predict success, countless hiring managers still use them to evaluate candidates:

EDUCATIONAL BACKGROUND

Not the school you went to, the degree or post-graduate degree you received, or your GPA provide a measurable edge in predicting success. Despite that, some companies establish arbitrary requirements as barriers to entry. All this does is limit their pool of potential candidates. Furthermore, studies show that most candidates—particularly women—who lack an advertised requirement will not apply for the job. Remember that Steve Jobs, Mark Zuckerberg, Michael Dell, and Bill Gates hold no college degrees...except for the honorary degrees they picked up after creating world-changing companies.

BRAINTEASERS

Why are manhole covers round? How many stoplights are in New York City? These types of questions, which were in fashion for a time, have proven to be largely useless in terms of predicting whether a candidate will perform well in a job. In its hiring, Google has even banned such questions after finding no correlation to the success of new hires.

INDUSTRY EXPERIENCE

There's a body of science that has overturned the commonly accepted folk wisdom that experience in an industry is predictive of success. It can be useful on the margin, of course, but I'll choose a Rockstar from another industry over a B-Player with ten years at my competitor in a heartbeat. In all but the most arcane roles and industries (yours likely isn't one of them), competencies are transferable.

INTERVIEW SKILLS

Some people may turn out to be terrible employees, but they shine in the interview. In fact, that is often the case—perhaps because the person has had to interview on a regular basis. The skills required to succeed in an interview are far different from those required of the job. Never forget that a great interview isn't necessarily a great hire, and vice versa.

GUT FEELINGS

We're all susceptible to our own biases, particularly affinity bias. No matter how much we talk about diversity, we tend to hire people similar to ourselves. Left to our own devices, we're more likely to hire someone who attended our alma mater, looks like us, and speaks like us. Within the first seconds of meeting a person, we make assessments and judgments—what Malcolm Gladwell calls "thin-slicing." Then, we spend the remainder of the interview confirming our biases. It's an evolutionary strategy that, in this case, works against our best interests. Without a standardized way to measure candidates, you will "feel good about this guy." If gut feelings were in any way accurate, I wouldn't have written this book.

SKIP STEPS ALTOGETHER

It's tempting to want to stop the recruiting process midway through because you think you've identified your Rockstar after a killer interview. "I've found our head of marketing," you announce. Because Rockstars represent the top 5 percent, logically, you won't be able to make that evaluation until you've seen a reasonable pool of applicants and until you've completed the all-important last stages of the process with your finalist. Every step of the process is crucial; there are no shortcuts. They're additive to reducing your risk of a mis-hire, or inversely, to improving your current 50 percent hiring accuracy up to 90 percent.

CHECK REFERENCES TOO LATE

This is a step that a lot of people put off—or worse, skip altogether—because it's time-consuming and requires coordination with others. Reference checking can be a reliable predictor in distinguishing Rockstars from Rockstar lookalikes. But only if you ask the right questions of the right people. It provides a wealth of information that should be factored into every hiring decision and is anything but a formality. And yet, many employers check references after they've already made their decision. Why bother?

THROW NEW HIRES INTO THE DEEP END

Some companies assume that Rockstars don't need time

to acclimate to their new surroundings, that they'll just hit the ground running. Rockstars, particularly senior-level managers, need time to adjust to their new reality, just like everyone else.

CHAPTER 2

DETERMINE YOUR COMPANY'S DNA

|||||||||||||||||||||||

Shortly after my twenty-sixth birthday, I created my first startup company, Career Central. It was 1995 in Silicon Valley, and this was among the first recruiting companies in the era of the burgeoning Internet. It sounds common today, but back then prospective clients asked us, "Huh? What's online recruiting?" Before we could recruit for our clients, however, we needed to recruit for ourselves. Even before we could do that, we had to decide who we were. What was the soul of our burgeoning company to be?

I needed to decide what I wanted the business to accomplish and what sort of company would be successful in Internet recruiting. Then, I began to think about the people who I would need on my team to bring about that success.

My founding team and I came up with three qualities that we knew we wanted in every one of our employees: tirelessness, selflessness, and fearlessness.

"Tireless" meant people willing to put in the hours, work hard, and move fast. Tireless people are driven and resilient in the face of challenges.

"Selfless" meant people who would work collaboratively but also adopt a servant mentality toward our clients. We wanted to differentiate our company from others by tripping over our own feet to serve customers; more than just being customer-focused, we wanted people who were hardwired to put others first.

Finally, we chose "fearless" because we knew we needed people who were unafraid of change and ambiguity. That's what any startup requires, of course, but we suspected the Internet recruiting category was going to evolve rapidly over time. It did; within two years, over 1,000 job website companies had launched.

Our work paid off. We had near-perfect retention of our employees, even in the late 1990s war for talent. Without a doubt, it's because we took such care to craft our company DNA early and to recruit only people who shared our hardwiring.

By 2000, our company had grown to 150 employees, and

client satisfaction was exceptionally high. That's when Spencer Stuart, one of the top-ranked executive search firms in the world, acquired our company. We had been able to deliver results because we had a great culture, which was the product of our deliberately acquiring people who shared the DNA we wanted on the team.

THE ROLE DNA PLAYS

Attracting Rockstars is one thing. Keeping them is another. That requires giving them a place to excel. Twenty-five years later, many of my former Career Central colleagues still tell me that it was the best job they've ever had.

The number one thing Rockstars look for is a challenge, be it a challenge in terms of career growth, trajectory, or job promotions. It's even more important than money. Whether you're the CEO or the leader of a department, your job is to create a culture that fosters and enables that.

According to a landmark study, 69 percent of people won't consider a job with a company that has a bad reputation; they won't even talk to them. Here's the kicker: This is true even among people who are unemployed.

Bad reputations develop when companies fail to foster a healthy culture. You can't fake it and you can't mask it with press releases or fancy websites. If you don't develop a winning culture—a place where Rockstars are compelled to join and a place where they can do their best work, you'll fail to recruit them. And if you do by chance get lucky and land a Rockstar, they'll quickly leave once they realize their mistake. So, if your culture isn't stellar, save your time and don't even proceed to Chapter 3. Recruiting isn't your biggest problem.

Be very clear about the DNA of your company so you know the people you'll need to hire. Your company's DNA isn't a long list of feel-good values—that gold emblazoned list of fifteen useless slogans mounted in the waiting room of most companies.

Rather, it's the three to five precise traits that you've identified as most important. You'll recall that ours at Career Central were "tirelessness," "selflessness," and "fearlessness." What are yours? If you don't identify them first, every step in this process that follows is *ipso facto*, a waste of time. You're going to great lengths to identify a person who shares your DNA. But if you don't know what your DNA is, how can you possibly know whether that person shares it?

In my companies, I've often hired people with the right DNA and subsequently found roles for them, rather than the other way around. Traditionally, companies identify the skillset they need and then hire people with those skills. The DNA of the person is often an afterthought, if it's considered at all. That's a recipe for diluting your culture and damaging your reputation. I know this sounds easy, but you must put DNA before experience, as so few companies do.

Retaining Rockstars is essential to an organization. Losing one is understandably devastating. To keep them, you must engage them with challenging work and an opportunity to succeed. Everyone wants to be an essential member of a winning team.

If you can provide that environment, your Rockstars won't even pick up the phone from a headhunter even if they're offering more money (and they usually are). A Glassdoor. com study showed that 84 percent of employees would consider leaving a job if a company with an excellent reputation (read: culture) called them. You can't afford to not be that company.

THE DIFFERENCE BETWEEN DNA AND CULTURE

When I interview a potential employee, I'm not looking at how that person will fit into the company's culture. I want people that will stand out—while still sharing the same core beliefs as the people they're joining. I don't want to hire people that look, speak, and act alike—a bunch of robots. Rather, I'm looking at their DNA. Do they have the three to five traits that we've identified as non-negotiable? If they do, they'll fit well enough—and hopefully be additive to the culture.

Culture is the collective makeup of a group of people, while DNA is a given individual's makeup. The latter is something we can assess a candidate against. To illustrate, consider an organ transplant. Sometimes, the body rejects the organ. The same thing can happen in a company when a new hire doesn't have the DNA that fits with the company. The "body" rejects the new "organ." If that happens, whether it's an employee who doesn't fit in a company or an organ that doesn't cooperate with a body, it won't take long to discover.

DNA, in its scientific sense, determines the color of our eyes and hair, and our height. For our purposes, I've expanded the definition to encompass everything that comprises a person, including how their personality and behavior is hardwired.

As previously noted, research indicates that our traits are baked into the cake at an early age—we simply are who we are. A recruiter's job is to put a candidate under a microscope and peer into that person's DNA. Are they detail-oriented? Passionate? Intensively creative? DNA guides behavior, and behavior determines whether an employee will live the values of the company and, ultimately, be successful in their role.

DNA is, in a sense, the soul of a company, and it shapes the resulting culture in intuitive and unspoken ways. Rather than a divinely handed-down set of well-articulated tableaus, it is, instead, an *a priori* set of guiding principles, an inherently understood morality that requires no discussion or explanation. It manifests itself in how things are done, what's expected, what's allowed, what's unacceptable, and how employees are punished and rewarded. It's how we communicate. It's how we act.

If you've done a good job of defining it, the DNA of your employees may evolve as it grows, but it won't radically change.

HOW TO FIND YOUR DNA

A clearly articulated DNA stands for something. It has a viewpoint. You must be willing to say, "This is what we are all about." And you must be willing to part ways with people, even top performers, who don't live the values you've articulated. Protect your company's culture—at all costs. Tony Hsieh, CEO of the Zappos division of Amazon, is notorious for exiting employees who don't match the company's core values—even offering them $2,000 in their first seven days to leave of their own volition.

It takes discipline to consistently adhere to this standard. There will always be pressure to settle, but remember: People can be coached and performance can improve, but DNA cannot be changed; it's immovable.

What happens when you make a bad hire and you realize

the DNA doesn't match? Kindly let the person go. You'll save both your company and the individual a lot of time and frustration. It's not a judgment. They're not a bad person—it was simply a mis-hire.

IDENTIFYING THE EXISTING DNA

If you're just starting a company and haven't yet hired anyone, this exercise will be easier because you haven't had the chance to make a hiring mistake.

But more than likely, you already have employees. To identify the DNA that already exists at your company, assemble your core team—the CEO and her key staff. These are typically members of the senior team, plus the head of HR or talent acquisition, and folks that are broad in their knowledge of the current employee base.

Have this team meet in person and ask them to identify three Rockstars already in the company (present company excluded, of course). These three people should epitomize the company, the ones who are the fabric of the company, who define its soul. These are the people who, if they gave their notice, would cause you to cry yourself to sleep.

Next, discuss the characteristics they have in common. List them out on the whiteboard. What DNA elements do they share? Are they driven? Fearless? Great problem-solvers?

Brainstorm everything you can think of. We're trying to get to the essence of what traits they share.

Organize this list into subcategories, grouping similar traits together. You are looking for three to five traits that define your company's DNA. It may take more than one session to figure out. Continue refining your results because the end product is the essence of your company. And your new recruiting standard.

Though it's better to do this when your company is still small (ten to 100 employees), it's never too late. I've facilitated this exercise for clients even when they have 5,000 employees. At that size, you may find that it varies from division to division.

COMMUNICATING THE DNA

Sharing the results, the essence of your company, is important. Create a plan to educate all members of your organization, regardless of their position. This is more than just a single email. It's an ongoing discussion.

Here's what to say: From this day forward, because these characteristics define our company, everyone we recruit must have all of these traits. Not three or four out of five. All of them. It's non-negotiable. Provide specific examples of what you mean by "Tirelessness." It's not simply the word.

It's the essence of the word and the expectations around it. What is revered? What behaviors will not be tolerated?

Be prepared because the day will soon come when an amazing candidate crosses your desk. He will have the numbers, the credentials, and the personality, but he won't share all five DNA qualities you've identified as non-negotiable. Do not hire him, regardless of the pressure placed upon you by your manager, your Board, or your team. Just say no.

Of equal importance, the second piece of the communication plan is more delicate and must be done one-on-one. You need to begin exiting employees who don't share the now-articulated DNA. Yes, this will undoubtedly be difficult. Some of these employees are top performers, some are in leadership positions, some have relationships with key customers. It doesn't matter. If you're serious about building a culture that attracts and keeps Rockstars, you must have consistency in your DNA.

Make the decision to part ways with them. You need not do it all in one day, and you won't do it inhumanely. Have a conversation and point out the disconnects; give examples of the lack of fit. It's easy to look the other way when an employee delivers results but doesn't share the DNA. This is where so many leaders fail. Don't be one of them.

Be very clear about why this is happening. Tell them that,

as a company that wants to grow, the culture needs to attract Rockstars. Explain that to attract Rockstars, you need a culture that is unstoppable, fun, and rewarding and where people can do their best work and be challenged. To do that, you need a team of people consistent in their DNA characteristics.

You'll find that people who don't share the DNA will realize their days are numbered, and that's okay. Some will leave of their own volition. The body is rejecting the cells. That's when you know your culture is becoming consistent.

LIVING THE DNA

Now, it's up to you, your CEO, your leadership team, and every manager in the company to ensure that employees are living the values of the company. Recognition is an important piece of this. When someone demonstrates the DNA of the company in a meaningful way, make a public example of them. Rewards are key, too—both financial and non-financial; we'll talk more about this later. If someone consistently lives the DNA of the company, promote them. This sends an important message that it's not only performance and results that matter.

When someone isn't living the DNA, it's often the chief talent officer or head of human resources who hears about it first. That person needs to ensure that the rest of the senior leadership team knows about the behavior. Just as your head of marketing serves as the guardian of your brand, the head of HR/talent is the guardian of your company's DNA.

That's why it's important that your head of HR/talent be one of your early hires. In my view, it's the single most critical hire a CEO can make. And I encourage my clients to make it one of their first twenty hires. They're often surprised by this, but when they do it, they're grateful that I was so insistent. It sends a message to everyone in the organization that recruiting Rockstars with similar DNA matters. That we put talent first. This person must report to the CEO, and must be the first and foremost example of the company's defined DNA.

You need not reinvent the wheel with all of this. Finding other companies with similar DNAs can give you ideas. Through research and asking around, you should be able to identify companies with like-minded values. Maybe you hire a lot of people from a particular company. Study what that company does. How do they live their DNA? What types of events, celebrations and promotions do they host? What is their talent strategy? What is their compensation design?

USING SALES & MARKETING TACTICS TO RECRUIT TALENT

Recruiters can learn a lot from the world of sales and marketing. The analogies are strikingly apparent and the principles are easily transferrable. I began my education and career as a marketer, so the more I learned about talent, the more I realized how similar attracting Rockstars is to attracting customers. See Exhibit 1 for some examples.

BRAND AWARENESS

Just as your company's products have a brand, so, too, does your company as an employer. It's how people think about your company and what it's like to work there. Market the hell out of your employer brand. Create stories to help prospective candidates visualize what it's like to work there. Use video to capture a sense of the company's DNA.

CANDIDATE PIPELINE

Develop a candidate pipeline in the same manner that a head of sales and marketing develops a customer pipeline. This pipeline is the bench of talent. Develop it before you need it. Just-in-time hiring is too slow and results in hasty decisions.

EMPLOYER VALUE PROPOSITION

When salespeople pitch a new product, they speak about the *product value proposition*, which is the value it delivers to the customer. An *employer value proposition* is the value the prospective employee receives from working at the company.

It's the career path, the challenge, the place where they can do their best work. That is the "product" you're selling to prospective employees.

COMPETITORS

Just as a salesperson keeps abreast of competing products, you need to study competing employers in your location and industry. Who are they? What are they offering? How do you differentiate yourself? Who is winning the war for the Rockstars, particularly in your city?

COMPENSATION

Just as each grocery store product has a price point, so, too, does talent: compensation. Marketers have pricing philosophy, and you need a compensation philosophy for decision making. That might mean being creative with fixed and variable forms of compensation, developing a hybrid of the two. It also means targeting up-and-comers for whom this is a meaningful move and pay increase, instead of an individual making a lateral move with the same compensation.

TARGET EMPLOYEE

Salespeople zero in on their target audience. Do you know specifically who your target employee is? Have you developed an avatar of that person? What's their DNA? What's their background? Where do they live? If you don't know who you're looking for, you're guaranteed not to find them.

CANDIDATE EXPERIENCE

Consider your candidate experience in the same way that sales and marketing execs consider customer experience. What's the first thing you see when you walk in the front door? The impact of your recruiting emails? The warmth of your receptionist's smile? When's the last time you conducted usability studies on the "Careers" section of your website? What's it like to interview here? What unique things do you do to make it an easy decision to say "Yes" to your offer? What's the onboarding plan to welcome new hires with open arms?

EMPLOYEE SURVEYS

Just as marketers survey customers about likes and dislikes, employee surveys open a dialogue to determine what's working and what isn't.

EXIT INTERVIEWS

Just as you conduct retention analysis when you lose a customer, conduct exit interviews with employees. Where did they go and why? What could you have done differently?

In this chapter, we've revealed that Rockstars value culture and challenge more than money. We've discussed the necessity of defining a companywide DNA to seek in employees, which will, in turn, contribute to a cohesive strong culture. Finally, we've used the tools of sales and marketing as a template for a recruiting philosophy.

In the next chapter, we'll begin the process of recruiting Rockstars. Remember, it doesn't make sense to proceed until you've done an honest assessment of your culture. I've got a free tool to do this—you can download it at www. RecruitRockstars.com/Bonus

Marketing & Sales   Recruiting Rockstars

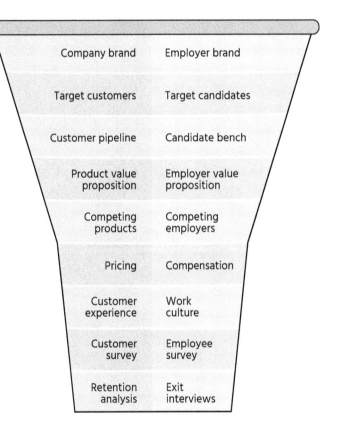

Marketing & Sales	Recruiting Rockstars
Company brand	Employer brand
Target customers	Target candidates
Customer pipeline	Candidate bench
Product value proposition	Employer value proposition
Competing products	Competing employers
Pricing	Compensation
Customer experience	Work culture
Customer survey	Employee survey
Retention analysis	Exit interviews

PART II

RECRUIT ONLY ROCKSTARS

CHAPTER 3

CREATING A JOB INVITATION

||||||||||||||||||||

Recruiting Rockstars requires more than a mere job description; it requires a *Job Invitation*.

Rockstars have countless career opportunities—their phones ring off the hook. So, only a compelling invitation will prompt them to engage in a conversation about your organization. A well-written invitation accomplishes the most important requirement of this phase of the recruiting process: It expands the funnel of potential candidates.

Two years ago, I worked with a client who was head of HR for a California consumer foods company that brought in $100 million each year. Despite that fact, my client never had enough candidates for open positions. I asked her to email me three of her job descriptions.

They were awful.

I was half-asleep by the second one. I'm not picking on her, to be clear: Ninety-nine percent of job descriptions I see are awful. They're dry, boring, and written entirely from the company's perspective.

Just as strong marketing copy draws in potential customers, well-crafted Job Invitations draw in prospective employees. A strong Job Invitation should scream: "You're going to love it here! You're going to do the best work of your life! You're going to have an opportunity to do things you care about! You're going to be challenged!"

My client's job descriptions were just the opposite. They focused on stringent requirements, which do nothing but eliminate people who might otherwise be a great fit. Bullet point after bullet point of, "You must have this, you must do that, don't even bother applying if you haven't…"

I encouraged my client to invest $100 for a copywriter to spend a few hours creating prose focused on the candidate, rather than her company. With her new Job Invitations, she was now inviting candidates to have a confidential conversation with her—so much more effective than boring job descriptions asking candidates to click the "Apply" button. In fact, this one change increased her candidate flow fivefold and shortened her recruiting cycle time by 30 percent.

A 2016 study by the Talent Board reveals that, during this initial recruitment phase, candidates are looking for three things:

1. An understanding of the company's culture.
2. Insight into what it's like to work there.
3. A personal connection to the brand.

WHAT DOES A JOB INVITATION LOOK LIKE?

Stop. You are no longer crafting job descriptions. From now on, you are creating Job Invitations for candidates to have a confidential discussion with you about your company. You may have a specific role in mind for that person, but the conversation needs to start even broader than that. You've got to get them to the table. Remind yourself: record-low unemployment. Phone ringing off the hook from headhunters. How do you entice them to engage for fifteen minutes about what you can offer? Think like a marketer.

The Job Invitation is the critical first step toward that discussion. It must be well-written, creative, compelling, and candidate-focused. Don't list requirements (which, as you'll soon learn, aren't predictive of much anyway). Requiring a candidate to have a particular college degree or a specific number of years of experience in a field only discourages potential Rockstars from applying. You're missing out on the best!

Here's proof. A 2014 *Harvard Business Review* study found that the majority of people will not apply for a job if they don't meet 100 percent of a job description's requirements. They take those requirements literally—they assume you're serious about them. Ironically, every day, I see my clients hire folks completely contrary to the original requirements. In that case, why start with those mandatories in the first place? Each requirement weeds out another batch of people, narrowing the field.

Recall that Rockstars prize three things most:

★ A challenging environment that allows for their best work
★ Professional and personal life balance
★ Job stability

In addition to creating an environment where great work can be done, think beyond the person as a mere candidate. Think of them first as a human—just like you and me. Flesh and blood. With worries, a mortgage to pay, kids to put through college, and a desire to make an impact on the world. Figure out how your company will enable that person to be self-actualized and find work-life integration. How does your company—its DNA and its leadership—allow people to have a great life, even outside of the work itself? The Job Invitation—and the ensuing discussion—must speak to the whole person, not just the candidate part of the person. This is part of why the formality of interviews is so deceptive—it belies the human vulnerabilities underneath. Both interviewer and candidate have their game faces on—it's no wonder that one out of two new hires bomb.

Stability and job security are admittedly trickier; job tenure is decreasing, jobs are increasingly being replaced by out-sourcing and automation, and the half-lives of companies are fleeting. Still, it's worth remembering that this is something top candidates seek and why you must educate candidates on why your company will still exist in five years.

So, here are vital components that will catch the attention of Rockstars:

- ★ Be clear about your company's identity and what it's truly like to work there. Capture the spirit, the energy, and collective enthusiasm for its mission.
- ★ Be up front about your non-negotiables, such as location, hours, and the like. But distinguish first what is literally non-negotiable and what isn't. Presume that candidates will take you literally at your word. These must-haves should be few, because for the Rockstar candidate, I'll bet that you're willing to flex on a whole lot of things.
- ★ Ask your current Rockstars to help create a compelling message. Why did you join us? Why do you stay? What's the most unique part of working here? How would you describe the experience? Their answers may surprise—or scare—you, but you need to hear them. Once you do, you

can attract more Rockstars by using that information. I've learned to treat this like market research with prospective customers and use their actual words in the Job Invitation.

★ Hire a copywriter, engage your head of marketing, and include links to videos (they need not be professionally produced—in fact, the less slick, the better) of current Rockstars sharing their experience.

★ Give the position a creative title. Rockstars want a title that reflects the importance of their work. Give it to them. Titles matter, and people act in accordance with the station to which they believe they belong; better to have them rise to a higher station than sink to a lower one. Director of Customer Service? Blah. Why not "Head of Making Customers Love Us?" I'd be interested in that one.

★ Make the "Careers" section of your website engaging. It should tell the story of who you are and what people can expect if they join your team. And—for God's sake—don't include an "Apply Here" button. Rockstars who are currently employed, don't apply. The button should say "Let's Talk" or "Let's Have a Conversation," and stress confidentiality.

All of this takes work. But it will be worth it. If you'd like to see an example of the Job Invitations I use with my clients, I'll give it to you for free. Just go to www.RecruitRockstars. com/Bonus for the download.

When I tackle a search for one of my clients, the first thing we do is brainstorm all the reasons the job is a phenomenal opportunity. I pull it out of them. "Give me more, more, more. How do I sell this to a Rockstar?" (If the list is short, I pass on the search because we'll never be able to bring Rockstars to the table.) The client is usually surprised by how great their opportunity actually is. We look for every compelling reason someone might want the role...things like equity, career path, the CEO's track record, ability to work with a great manager, unique aspects of the culture, or the fact that it's a high-growth industry. Ping pong tables no longer suffice. Dig deep to identify reasons that this role and your company will appeal to Rockstars.

I've learned that video is the perfect way to tell the story. Consider including a link from the invitation to a short video in which the hiring manager discusses the kind of person that she is seeking, and why the job is a great opportunity. Include a tour of the office—anything to help sell the company.

The invite doesn't have to be long; if it takes more than a page or two to tell your company's unique story, you don't know what your story is. Solve that before crafting your Job Invitation.

All of this matters because you can't consistently find Rockstars in a timely manner if you don't have enough candidates in your pipeline at all times. The I'll-know-it-when-I-see-it approach is doomed from the start. It will ultimately result in a narrow pipeline, which is the most common cause of failure at this stage of the process. If you don't have a compelling Job Invitation, your pipeline will starve, and there won't be a sufficient pool of people from which to choose.

DEFINE THE JOB VALUE PROPOSITION

Heads of marketing invest months researching and developing a Customer Value Proposition. Then, they obsessively hand-craft the words to tell that story. The same applies in recruiting Rockstars. You, your head of talent, and your leadership team must research and refine a compelling Job Value Proposition. Why should Rockstars want to "purchase" your job opportunity? Why should they choose to invest their precious years working for you?

There are two components to the Job Value Proposition. One aspect is that of your company—its mission, passion, growth trajectory, etc.—and why your offerings are more compelling than those of your candidate's current employer.

The second aspect is that of the specific role. The position is secondary to the company, of course, because jobs have become so fluid. It's important to show that the company is going places, and that the person who fills the job will be an essential part of the growth path. This isn't just a job; it's an investment in the ownership of something meaningful and rewarding. This is a bus you simply need to be on. And we'll find the right seat together.

Rockstars want ownership. They want an ostensible, tangible thing that bears their signature. They need to make an impact. They crave a yardstick by which to be measured. That's precisely why you want Rockstars on your team. While others shrink from responsibility, Rockstars demand it. So, ensure that the Job Value Proposition reflects that ownership—for what piece of the enterprise will they own or be held to account?

PLACE THE JOB IN A LARGER CONTEXT

I've read job descriptions where not only is the description awful, but the *job* itself is awful. A Rockstar won't do that work. So, you seemingly have two choices: either settle by hiring a lesser talent or change the job. That's a false dilemma. If you're serious about creating a Rockstar culture, change the job. Twist it, morph it, expand it. Do something to make it a meaty and challenging role. This may mean adding responsibilities to a position, eliminating inconsequential or inessential aspects, or merging it with another job. It's far better to redraw a job than to dilute—or, if you prefer, *pollute*—your company culture.

Even an assembly line job can be made more challenging and meaningful. Rockstars can measure performance on an assembly line; they can find the challenge of fixing a broken line or improving a functioning one. Instead of treating them like a product on that assembly line, treat them like someone who has an ownership stake in its evolution.

Whether it's widgets or financial auditing or turning around a sales territory, your Rockstar candidate needs to know they are being sought for their creative problem-solving skills. They'll be put in a challenging environment that will demand their best work to make things faster, better, smarter, and cheaper. Tie this particular job to the role of its department and to the larger company's growth plan. Show your candidate the trajectory of their own career within the company. That's how you woo a Rockstar every time.

NON-NEGOTIABLE DNA REQUIREMENTS

Without the proper DNA match, your new hire has a zero percent chance of success. So, a non-match has no place in a candidate pipeline. Weed out mismatches from the beginning. Whatever words you've chosen to represent your DNA, clearly spell them out in the Job Invitation to alert candidates that these qualities are a must. (And that during the ensuing process, you're going to thoroughly vet and reference check them, so let's not waste each other's time.)

COMPETENCIES

Competencies are another piece of the Job Invitation. Rather than arcane requirements that aren't predictive of success, we'll include the five to ten competencies that are necessary to do the job well. As part of your Scorecard, you already developed the key candidate qualities. These belong in the Invitation.

This is time well spent. The Job Invitation is used throughout the recruiting process, from job posts to phone screen to interview to offer. It is the touchstone of the role.

In this chapter, we've discussed the need to "sell" both your company and the particular position to candidates. We've replaced job descriptions with Job Invitations, which are indispensable in recruiting. The invite explains the compelling reasons why a Rockstar would want to work with you in the job you're offering. It explains what the role entails and how it fits into the company as a whole and plays a part in its growth strategy. It explains the non-negotiable DNA fit that you seek. It also notes the necessary competencies that a candidate will possess to succeed in that capacity.

In sum, the Job Invitation answers two questions: "What must the candidate offer the company?" and "What does the company offer the candidate?" Virtually every company's job specs focus simply on the former. Don't let your company be one of them.

In the next chapter, we'll explore the best sources for finding Rockstars.

CHAPTER 4

TAP INTO THE BEST SOURCES

||||||||||||||||||||||||

When I work with clients, the ultimate goal of our recruiting process is to complete the search with two solid Rockstars so ideally suited that it's difficult to choose between them (the second candidate is an insurance policy). Locating that pair of ideal candidates, of course, is no easy task. This chapter will make it substantially easier.

A former client, the CEO of a mid-sized industrial manufacturing company, faced this recurring problem of a dry candidate pipeline. His job descriptions were dull and painful, and he posted them on all the major job-seeker sites. There's nothing wrong with that, but it's not a solid sourcing strategy, especially in times of low unemployment. It's "Post & Pray."

We improved his Job Invitations by hiring a copywriter and focusing on the candidate, not the company, as explained in Chapter 3. We also created an employee referral program—more on that shortly—and I taught him how to activate his own network.

The results were incredible. He tripled his flow, which shortened his recruiting cycle. More importantly, it gave him confidence that he had a qualified pool of candidates, which dramatically increased his success rate in hiring Rockstars.

HOW MANY FROGS MUST YOU KISS?

Time and time again, in search after search, I've found that 150 is the magic number. The way you build that pool is by sourcing. Your head of sales needs to fill the pipeline with enough prospective customers, based on her close-rate, to ensure that she hits her number each month. So, too, you must fill your candidate pipeline with enough potentially qualified and interested candidates. It sounds obvious, but my clients often starve the pipeline and the searches drag on forever. That's when they call me.

Locating a Rockstar is like panning for gold: You're going to sift through some mud to find that rare shiny gem. It's a formula that looks like this:

150 POTENTIAL CANDIDATES

↓

20 VIABLE CANDIDATES

↓

5 VETTED CANDIDATES

↓

2 OUTSTANDING FINALISTS

↓

1 ROCKSTAR HIRE

What this means is that 150 résumés, LinkedIn profiles, or referrals will yield approximately twenty candidates worth talking to. That first number isn't arrived at arbitrarily; it has proven time and again to be the optimally sized pool to produce a successful result.

As defined earlier, Rockstars are the top 5 percent of candidates who have the desired competencies and DNA, at the budgeted compensation level. It stands to reason that there's a 1-in-20 probability that a given individual will be of that caliber. This group represents candidates with Rockstar potential. It's still too early to identify anyone as such, so guard against falling in love with a terrific LinkedIn profile.

Remember that it is just that: *feeling*. We have a hypothesis that this candidate has potential—but it's nothing more. There's a saying in professional football: "You can't win the Super Bowl in September, but you *can* lose it."

We'll use an effective phone conversation to simultaneously court and assess the list of twenty individuals, and narrow it to five people whom you believe may fit your company in terms of competency and culture. These five will be invited to interview. Because that is a time-intensive process, I err on the side of caution. I don't provide interviews on a whim, nor should you.

From that group of five, you'll identify the two best fits, one of whom you'll provide with a can't-refuse offer.

SOURCING STRATEGY

So, how do you find these twenty viable candidates? I've tried every way imaginable and have concluded that these are the best ways in terms of cost, yield, and speed.

PERSONAL NETWORKING

Ideally, 20 percent of your hires should be sourced from your personal network. You likely believe that you're already tapping out your network, but I'll bet you can do more and it's the single best use of your recruiting time.

Let's be specific. The first place you should look is your own circle of contacts. This doesn't mean hiring friends and family—I could write a separate book on the perils of that strategy. Instead, it means asking trusted people you know for referrals. These are people you already know, who want you to succeed, and who may know others that would be a good fit with your organization. These are the people in your life who would do anything for you. Now's the time to ask for the favor.

Your personal network is more than just your friends and family. Consider approaching people you know in your industry, members of your church and professional organizations, reporters who cover the industry, your customers, your vendors, your neighbors, your attorney, your accountant, your dentist. I once hired a brilliant young sales rep—the son of one of my mom's friends—who became a Rockstar. Wrack your brain to pinpoint the 100 to 200 people in your life who might invest a bit of time to be a talent scout for you.

The key, however, is to make it easy for them. Be concise about the person you're looking for. Don't ask: "Who do you know?" They know a lot of people—it's too hard. Rather, ask: "Who's the best software sales rep you've met in the past year?" or "Who's the best product manager you've worked with here in Denver?"

When you ask specific questions, a handful of folks in

your personal network will quickly think of several names without feeling burdened. The results will surprise you. Sometimes, they can introduce you; other times, they can't. But even just a name is useful. It's a lead. So, don't rule out anyone.

Always ask if you can use their name when reaching out to the person they referred—you're far more likely to have your email or call returned. Be sure to thank them whether you hire the person they referred or not, and always close the loop. Circle back with: "I spoke with her. Here was the outcome…" If you skip this step, don't be surprised if it's the last introduction they make.

I recommend focusing your outreach locally. Because the vast majority of vacancies are filled with local candidates, target your networking the same way.

REFERRALS FROM YOUR EMPLOYEES

This is the big one. Now that you've tapped into your own network, it's time to ask your employees to do the same. Best-in-class companies generate 50 percent of their hires from this single source, yet most companies achieve less than half this rate.

Employee referrals are the Holy Grail of recruiting. They deliver the highest quality of candidates, the shortest duration of search time, and the lowest cost-per-hire. The reason is simple: Rockstars attract Rockstars. That's why Rockstar cultures get stronger and stronger, just like a hurricane's center, tightening as the storm makes its march toward land.

Soliciting and acting on referrals from current employees generates goodwill and increases morale. Alternatively, if you aren't receiving employee referrals, you either have a culture problem or an employee referral program that's not working correctly. Only two-thirds of companies have employee referral programs, and most don't work as they should.

To make your employee referral program successful, keep it fresh. Make it exciting, interesting, and relevant. It should be a marketing program with a unifying theme. Tell your employees that you want their help in making this the best possible place to work: "We're going to be successful as a company. We're going to attract Rockstars. That's going to help create even more career opportunities."

Pay your employees for their successful referrals, but don't overthink the amount. Pay what you can (it's money well spent), whether that's $500, $1,000, $2,000, or even $10,000. Don't break the bank, though. If you can't afford cash, use stock, vacation time, trips, or gift cards. Be creative, but provide a reward.

Google conducted a recent study in which they doubled

their referral bonus from $2,000 to $4,000, and it didn't significantly impact the number of referrals.

Some companies pay different bonuses for different types of roles. I see this often when I recruit for my Silicon Valley clients. A company might pay $5,000 for an employee referral for a software engineer role, but $2,500 for an employee referral for any other position. The argument is that software engineers are harder to find, so a referral is worth more. The problem with this method is the message it sends to the rest of the organization. It says, "We value those people more." It is a dangerous, slippery slope. We know from the Google study that the amount you pay isn't the driver of the number of referrals you'll get. So, determine the highest amount that you can afford to pay as a referral bonus and be consistent with it across the board.

To get the most out of your employee referral program, promote the program often and keep it fresh. I refresh employees about our program at least once every month. Use email, posters, company meetings, occasional contests, and other vehicles to spread the word. Nothing is more effective than the CEO making personal mention of the program.

Keep it simple for employees. Don't make them do too much work. Just as when you ask your personal network for help, be specific and concise with what you're asking of your employees. You want to open the funnel, not close it.

Once you receive an employee referral, it's golden. Advance that person to the top of the stack. These people should be considered before anyone else, regardless of your initial instinct. And 100 percent of them must be at least phone screened because these are your best leads.

At most companies, employees won't receive a referral bonus until the employee they referred has been working for three or six or twelve months. A practice that I've found works particularly well is instantly rewarding the specific behavior we're trying to drive. What if you gave them a $10 Starbucks gift card right away, though, for each referral? That actually rewards the behavior you're seeking. Give them a gift card right away, plus pay out the bonus when the person is hired. Rewards tied to controllable outcomes work best.

Be careful about information that goes into a black hole. If you fail to follow through with referrals and then circle back to the referring employee, don't expect to receive more. When employee referrals are generating 50 percent of your hires, this often-overlooked administrative task becomes a great use of time.

An invaluable way to solicit additional names is to meet with every one of your new hires within their first thirty days and go through their Rolodex or LinkedIn network together. Literally sit with them and help them brainstorm who they might know that you should be talking to—for a current role, or a future one. You're looking for the names of the best people they've ever worked with. Be specific and say: "We are looking for sales reps and software developers. Who are the best you've worked with? And can you introduce me to them?"

You're not asking them to do much work, yet it's hugely beneficial. When you reach out to that person, ask, "Did you know that so-and-so just started working here? He told us that we'd be crazy not to talk to you. I'd love to set up a time to sit down with you and tell you what we're building."

Employee referrals cost less, take less time, have longer retention, and are likely to improve your company's culture because Rockstars aspire to work with the Rockstars they refer. Regardless of your current percentage of new hires referred by your employees, commit to increasing it by 50 percent in the next twelve months.

ONLINE JOB BOARDS

I have nothing against online job boards. I started one of the first ones back in 1995. In fact, they'll likely comprise 10 percent of your hires. But in a market with record-low unemployment, the fact is that you just won't reach many Rockstars this way. They're simply not combing through job postings as they once did.

Because responding to job boards has become increasingly easy for candidates—just click "Apply" and "Apply" and "Apply"—it no longer behaves as the filter it once was. That said, it's still worth a modest investment, particularly for lower-level jobs, and as part of your multi-pronged sourcing strategy.

But be sure to use a Job Invitation, not a boring job description, as discussed in the last chapter. Give your Job Invitation a title that will grab attention, much like a captivating email subject line. If it breaks through the clutter, far more people are likely to consider the role. A candidate sifting through job postings sees the same titles over and over again. When one is different, they're far more likely to click on it.

Which job boards are worth using? There are the well-known boards such as LinkedIn, CareerBuilder, and Indeed. Go ahead and use one. But lately, I find that I have the most success with niche job boards specific to an industry, function, or location. There are thousands of job boards for every conceivable job type you can imagine. Every trade magazine has a job board on their website. Even though the traffic is far less on the niche boards, they're worth testing because you'll reach the most targeted candidates.

Because it's so easy for people to apply online, I look for candidates who seek to differentiate themselves in some way. I notice insightful applicants, who have taken the time to make it clear that they're applying because of a genuine interest, connection to our mission, or understanding of what we do. "Dear Sir" goes directly to my trash.

A final note: acknowledge all applications. I don't expect you to do this personally. But even the most basic applicant tracking systems can now provide automated replies, thanking the candidate for their application and adding them to a "keep in touch" list. Somehow, acknowledge your applicants. Some of them are Rockstars and will be right for you in the future. And each of them knows other Rockstars—you can't afford for them to badmouth your company's poor manners.

GLASSDOOR

If you're not up to speed on Glassdoor.com, you're missing a beat. This is the website where people leave anonymous reviews of what it's like to work at—or interview with—your company. Go ahead and take a look. I'll wait.

(Un)fortunately, Glassdoor has become the first place that people look when deciding to even speak with a company. That's troublesome because anyone can post a review on Glassdoor, even people who potentially never even worked at the company. There's no vetting process and it takes an act of God to have a review removed.

The best way to combat this is by asking people who are doing well at your company to leave a positive review. Don't force them, of course, or entice them with incentives. It must be genuine and heartfelt. When reminding them about your employee referral program each month, just mention Glass-door. Suggest: "By the way, we know from our research that the first place that Rockstars go is Glassdoor. So, if you feel inclined to help us spread the word by leaving a review, that would be great. It takes thirty seconds, and we'd be really grateful." Don't specify "positive review." Their review needs to be pure and unvarnished, and you need to hear the truth anyway—no matter how much it hurts.

OTHER SOURCES

The final 20 percent of your hires should come from other sources: boomerang hires—people who return to your com-pany after leaving—headhunters, and other creative ways. In fact, I've tracked a list over the years of the wildest places that I've snagged Rockstars. I'm happy to share it with you—download it free from www.RecruitRockstars.com/Bonus

With regard to boomerangs, it's important to welcome returning employees. They often leave in search of greener pastures, only to discover the grass was greener back home. These people are invaluable because they discourage others from following suit. This is why it is also crucial that they're allowed to leave on good terms whenever possible. Burning bridges is just bad business anyway. Don't show your hurt feelings when they leave—keep the door open.

While we're at it, let's talk a bit about working with head-hunters because they're likely going to help you fill at least some of your vacancies.

THE INSIDER'S GUIDE TO OUTSIDE RECRUITERS

If you hire an outside recruiter (executive search consul-tant, headhunter, call us what you will), choose one that truly adds value. There are 90,000 recruiters in the United States, but sadly, many of them add little value to the pro-cess. Plus, they're expensive. Most recruiters charge 20 to 33 percent of the candidate's first-year compensation. If they're truly adding value by tracking down and vetting candidates, they're worth every penny. However, identifying candidates—the first phase of the recruiting process—has become so much easier, thanks to LinkedIn and the Internet.

That wasn't so thirty years ago, when it was difficult just to identify prospective candidates. Then, a headhunter had to "smile and dial" all day long, calling companies to try to identify people who might be good candidates. It took countless hours.

Fast-forward to today. The candidate-identification phase is the easiest part of the process. I can generate a list of people in two hours. Anyone can. The hard part is sifting through the list, assessing candidates, interviewing, vetting candi-dates, completing reference checks, and negotiating the offer.

As with job boards, niche recruiters who specialize in a certain area are often a better choice than a recruiter from a large generalist firm. Though the large search firms have well-deserved reputations and solid training programs, you can find individual recruiters who spun off from the big firms and now specialize. They will often be a better choice. In addition, you'll avoid the restrictions or off-limits lists of the big firms (they can't touch candidates from any of their current or recent clients). So, small-time recruiters can deliver big-time results.

HOW TO SPOT A GREAT RECRUITER

Ask your investors and Board members. Ask other CEOs. But don't pick from a Google listing. You are outsourcing a crucial function. How can you find a Rockstar candidate unless you find a Rockstar executive recruiter? You need a recruiter who knows what they're doing. Your recruiter should have a methodology and a high standard of assessing talent. Speak with a few before selecting one.

Here are the questions you should ask:

★ What are their metrics? What's the completion rate? What percentage of searches is actually completed? Numbers in the 80 to 90 percent range are strong. (If it sounds too good to be true, it probably is.)
★ What's their stick rate? A recruiter's stick rate is the per-

centage of candidates still in place after two years. Eighty percent or higher is a good starting point, since twenty-four months is the current national average for job tenure with a company.

★ What's their speed? On average, how many days does it take them to complete a search? The national average is ninety to 120 days. An efficient recruiter who isn't overloaded with searches can often do it in half that time.

★ What's their volume? Ask how many searches they're currently conducting. Literally find out their capacity. You want to know if your search will be one of fifteen they're working on, or one of three. Some recruiters limit the number of searches they take on, so they can give each one a lot of attention.

★ Who will be doing the work? You may hire a firm, but you must know specifically who will be conducting your search. Who will do the research to develop the list of potential candidates, and what tools will they use? Who will reach out to candidates—is it someone who will get their calls returned because they have a reputation with Rockstars? Is it someone who is creative and smart about how to message the opportunity? Are they persistent?

★ What is their vetting method for candidates? You'll want them to assess based on the competencies and DNA you're seeking. One of the first things you'll do with an executive recruiter is talk about the Scorecard, the competencies, and the DNA fit. Who will do the interviews? How many rounds of interviews? Will the interviews be in person, on the phone, or via Skype video?

★ What's their recruiting methodology? Focus on selecting a recruiter who recruits consistent with your philosophy.

★ Do they have an off-limits list? Usually, a recruiter doing a search for a company will agree not to recruit anyone out of that company for another client for a certain period of time, usually a year or two. The bigger the firm you work with, the more clients they have, and the longer that off-limits list grows.

★ How will they position your company and your opportunity? You want to break through the noise. To attract Rockstar candidates, you need to differentiate your company and the opportunity. Ask the potential recruiter what the message will be and how it will be compelling.

★ Will they provide visibility and transparency? Does the recruiter provide a weekly report and phone call on the candidates they've contacted? If they use an applicant tracking system (and just about everyone does), you should receive a weekly report of the entire pipeline—showing who's been contacted, who they've spoken with, who they've vetted, etc.

★ Do they offer a replacement guarantee? If a candidate doesn't work out, how long will a recruiter guarantee that placement? Guarantees range from one month to one year. A lot can go wrong in a year; not much can go wrong in a month. This guarantee is worth something, especially when investing a hefty search fee.

Have a variety of search firms on speed dial. Don't automatically use a go-to firm for every search; choose based on the type of search you need. It's difficult for a recruiter to be an expert and simultaneously have the capacity to take on all your searches.

PAYING A RECRUITER

There are three basic types of fee structures: contingency, retainer, and hybrid.

Contingency

This fee structure requires that you pay only when the hire happens. While it sounds like a bargain, it actually has many downsides. If a recruiter doesn't get paid until the candidate she found gets hired, she will be more likely to throw résumés against the wall and see what sticks. She'll also be inclined to invest less time on each step of the process: research, outreach, interviewing, and vetting. Contingency pay also incentivizes headhunters to give up when the going gets tough and spend their time on easier projects where they have a higher chance of getting paid. They neglect to mention this, so while you think your search is being handled, they've sometimes moved on to another one in the queue.

Retainer

This method means that you pay regardless of a successful search. You are essentially locking in the consultant's time. The downside of this structure is that it can lead to a lack of alignment of incentives because they are getting paid despite the outcome, and duration. Searches often drag for months and months. Because you can't see the actual time invested by the recruiter on your particular search, the fee structure can conflict with incentive.

Hybrid (Often Called "Container")

In this model, you pay a portion of the fee up front and the remainder after the search is complete. In my twenty-five years of working with—and leading—search firms, I've found this to be the ideal model because it leaves enough on the table to keep the recruiter focused, engaged, and motivated, yet there's enough of an up-front fee to lock in their time and attention on your assignment.

Regardless of structure, most recruiters charge a percentage of the total estimated first-year cash compensation (base + bonus + any other cash components). Typically, this ranges from 20 percent to 33 percent, the latter being the going rate for executive hires. Record-low unemployment rate means record-high fees and demand for headhunters. So, they should always be the last resort, after you've tapped out your own network and the previously mentioned sources.

But once you've exhausted your sources, engage a recruiter. The cost of a vacancy is far higher than the fees of an outside search consultant. What is that vacant sales territory in Atlanta costing you?

GETTING THE MOST OUT OF YOUR RECRUITER

Once you've made a selection, here are tips for working with your recruiter:

★ Hold your recruiter accountable, just as you would any employee or consultant. Because you're not the only client, you're competing for their time. That means being a squeaky wheel. Otherwise, the recruiter's largest long-term clients will remain on the front burner.

★ Invest time up front to set expectations. You'll want to define the role, create the Scorecard together, and determine how they'll assess candidates. Educate them about the industry, your company's culture, and the competencies required for the role. Arm them with data to overcome candidate objections.

★ Provide specific feedback on candidates they present to you. The more precise you are, the more they can refine the search. It's useless to tell your recruiter, "I really liked him!" You need to convey whether the competencies were a match, the DNA was a fit, etc.

★ In the war for talent, speed matters. It's critical that you promptly provide feedback to the recruiter when you consider or interview a candidate. My slowest clients lose amazing talent by dragging their feet.

WHEN SHOULD YOU BEGIN SOURCING?

This is a trick question. The answer is never stop sourcing. You're always hiring, which is why I insist that my clients invest 30 to 50 percent of their time on talent. You are proactively building a talent pipeline *ahead* of the need. Just-in-time hiring no longer works. When someone quits and there's a vacant seat, the clock is against you. If you haven't built up your pipeline before then, you are more likely to settle for a warm body.

I recommend forecasting your hiring needs for the next two years. How many people will you need, and in what roles? Your talent strategy should be a derivative of your business strategy. Are you doubling your salesforce over the next year? Where is the growth going to be? What functions, what levels, what types of jobs?

Focus on the areas in which you anticipate the most growth and begin building a pipeline. Remember, you need on average 150 qualified candidates per Rockstar hire, so the numbers can be daunting. If you're going to fill twenty positions, you'll need to look at 3,000 candidates. That's why it's crucial to build the pipeline of candidates ahead of the need. Unless you're a name-brand employer—Facebook, Tesla, Amazon—Rockstars aren't beating a path to your door.

Furthermore, don't forget about natural attrition. Your projections need to account for your turnover rate as well. One hundred employees with 20 percent turnover means you're hiring twenty employees this year just to stay even. Where will they come from?

I help my clients create a Candidate Relationship Management program, often in the form of an email newsletter—just as they have for their prospective customers. We're always growing the list of recipients. Through this every-other-week email, we remind potential candidates about our company and what we're doing. We include news about the company, funding, new customers, new hires, evidence that the industry is taking off.

Over time, this tool is often enough for people to raise their hand and say they're interested in learning more. It's also an effective way to stay in touch with candidates you've identified who haven't yet decided to engage, for whatever reason. You're dripping on them every other week.

You should also meet regularly with promising candidates—even if you don't have a specific job for them today. Have two of those meetings each week to continue building your pipeline. The people you invest time with are also good people to tap for candidate referrals.

To do all this, LinkedIn should become your best friend. Its Advanced Search function allows you to track down just about anyone. In fact, it's the most robust database of people in the world. Even though not quite everyone is in there and not every profile is completely up to date, it's become the essential tool that I use to find Rockstars.

Reach out to the people you want to get to know. Don't be pushy or arrogant. Don't send them a laborious job description. Instead, say: "I want to share our story with you" or "I'd love to speak for fifteen minutes." It's an invitation mindset. You'll be surprised how many people will engage in that kind of discussion. Rockstars, in particular, are always thinking about career progression. Used correctly—in a non-solicitous transactional way—LinkedIn opens a world of potential candidates.

Time is your most precious asset. That's why it's vital to be selective about the people you invest your time with. Train your hiring managers to do the same. When I see a résumé or a LinkedIn profile, I ask myself whether the person is worth twenty minutes of my time. The reality is that recruiting takes a lot of time—vetting, researching, referencing—which is why you sometimes hire an outside recruiter. You either pay in time (yours) or money (to a recruiter) when it comes to recruiting.

Recall that we talked about wanting 150 candidates in our

funnel for a given vacancy. Typically, we can eliminate 130 of those off the bat; they're just too far off the mark. That may mean we have some false-negatives, but we have to start somewhere. It begins to narrow the field to twenty. So, how do we separate the wheat from the chaff?

Referrals from my personal network, employees, investors, and my Board always get first priority. They are the best use of time. Remember, half of your hires should come from your employee referral program. So, they get the first call.

After that, you'll have before you a stack of résumés, bios, and LinkedIn profiles. Some detailed, some sparse. So, the question becomes how to narrow the field to the twenty that I'd most like to speak with. If I'm going to invest twenty minutes each, for a total of seven hours, I'm looking for some evidence—something, anything—that they might have the competencies I defined earlier. We need to start somewhere.

I look for markers that may indicate a person is a top-performer. No résumé will tell me that the person is a Rockstar. A résumé is nothing more than a sales brochure, but here are a few tips to weed through them:

★ Look at *résumés in batches*, rather than one at a time. You're only spending time with twenty candidates, so working in batches helps you compare and contrast across them. What initially may seem like a promising candidate on paper may pale in comparison to others I haven't yet seen. So, I hold off before reaching out to begin scheduling conversations until I've reviewed the entire batch.

★ Look for *specific quantified accomplishments or achievements*—growing sales, growing markets, turning around brands. Those are important markers of Rockstars because Rockstars deliver results; they make things happen and they are interested in telling you about those results. That doesn't mean that the résumé that lists job responsibilities, rather than quantified results, isn't a Rockstar, but the odds are far lower.

★ Look for *evidence of progression*. That could be in the form of increasing scope of responsibility, in promotions (particularly within a company, not just from one company to another) or in expansion of scope of duties (did their team expand?). The inverse is true, too. When I see stagnation, it could be because the person is not a Rockstar. Or maybe they once were, but their star is beginning to fade. I'm unlikely to invest precious time on them either. I want rising stars on my client's teams.

★ Look for *tenure with companies*. How long has a candidate been at their current job? If you've got a candidate who hops from job to job, staying less than two years at each position, let them go. Don't waste your time. Consider what I call the 3:10 Rule. I'm looking for people who have worked for three or fewer companies in the past ten years. Commonly, I'll see candidates who spent two years at each employer over the course of ten years. That's five employers, and in my book, that's too many. It tells me that the candidate either made bad choices about where to work or the company didn't see them as having enough value to retain their services and advance them through the organization. While the days of lifetime employment are over, the winnowing must start somewhere.

★ Finally, pay attention to the presentation. How clear is the résumé or profile? This should be the candidate's best work. If it has mistakes, it concerns me. If they've written a cover letter, is it compelling and authentic and insightful, or cliché and typo-ridden? Fewer than 5 percent of candidates provide an outstanding, thoughtful résumé or LinkedIn profile. It's a shame, but it's a great time-saver because Rockstars sweat the details.

Okay, next step. It's time to reach out to those that look most promising. If they applied for the position, it's relatively easy. They're hoping for the call. So, make it. I send an email letting them know that I'd like to schedule a twenty-minute intro call (I block out thirty in my calendar). I make three attempts: an email, then a call, and then a text.

But if the individual didn't apply for the position, they're a passive job seeker. So, before reaching out, I do everything possible to secure a personal introduction (using second-degree connections on LinkedIn—people who know both them and me). The response rate is far higher. Failing that, I do everything I can to get—or guess—their email address, inferring it from other folks I know at their company. If not, I send them a LinkedIn InMail, which will send them a note without revealing their email address. It takes a little bit of homework, but I've got this process down to about a minute each.

So, what does the note say? It's a super short invitation to have a brief discussion. Kiss first, before proposing marriage.

The subject line is simply "Confidential."

And the email or text or Inmail reads:

Hi Jack,

Your background is quite compelling. I've just been retained to recruit a remarkable Chief Revenue Officer for a fast-growing, private equity-backed company. With $50M revenues, it's the nation's leader in selling automotive after-market services. The role reports directly to the CEO, and leads a national organization of thirty sales reps. The CRO will receive meaningful equity in the company. Would you be open to a twenty-minute conversation? I'd appreciate the chance to discuss it with you.

Warmly, Jeff

In my experience, outreaching to thirty or so of the right

prospects with a short note will typically yield twenty phone conversations.

In this chapter, we talked about sourcing, including tips on how to use outside recruiters, how to narrow our list of candidates, the importance of always recruiting, and how to best spend your sourcing time.

In the next chapter, we'll look at interviewing so that we can narrow the field of twenty candidates down to five.

CHAPTER 5

INTERVIEW TO PREDICT SUCCESS

|||||||||||||||||||||

When it comes to interviewing, remember two key things:

1. A résumé is nothing more than a sales brochure. Use it to decide who you might want to interview—after that, its value is minimal.
2. Executed poorly, interviews are a lousy tool for predicting who will succeed at your company.

A client of mine, the CEO of a professional services company, was struggling to hire talented people. Like most executives, her success rate was about 50/50. It seemed like a weekly task of firing the mis-hires, which was not only a disruption to business but also emotionally exhausting.

I asked her if I could sit in on a few of her interviews. She hesitated, insistent that she had interviewed countless candidates over the years. I promised not to say a word, just to observe. She obliged. I sat in on a handful of her interviews, only to discover that her interviews were unstructured, almost haphazard. She was ill-prepared, random in her approach, talking far too much, making up questions on the fly. She was making almost every interviewing mistake in the book.

Interviews must be structured and consistent from one candidate to another. Together, we created a clear sequence of standardized predictive questions, and a year later, 75 percent of her hires are keepers. In other words, she improved her success rate by 50 percent.

Interviewing is where recruiting falls apart for most people. Too many hiring managers rely only on interviews and, frankly, those interviews stink. Don't believe me? You've been a candidate during your career—on the other side of the table. How many times can you remember being impressed by the discipline and forethought of the interviewer grilling you? Not often, I'll bet.

NON-PREDICTIVE TRAITS

Years ago, recruiting and interviewing were black magic. The science just didn't exist. But fast-forward to today; there are countless studies that have correlated hiring factors to candidate success. We can actually look at what is predictive and what's not. So, why would we possibly use the latter? Simple. You've been too busy to find out. I've dug up and examined every study that's been done.

Turns out, executives tend to focus on many characteristics that have little to no ability to forecast the success of a candidate. So, what are those traits? Some will surprise you.

INDUSTRY EXPERIENCE

Experience within an industry is, of course, nice to have but isn't sufficient by itself to predict a candidate's success. I'll take the right DNA any day of the week and teach the new hire my industry. It also turns out that candidates from the industry—even from a direct competitor—often bring bad habits with them, and poor assumptions about the industry. They just have a different world view. The fresh perspective of an outsider—of course, with the right competencies and DNA—is a better bet in almost every case. Not to mention, there are no hassles with non-compete agreements. Don't make the mistake of assuming that because a candidate worked in your industry, they will succeed at your company.

EDUCATION

Nor does it matter where someone went to school or what

their GPA was. Just because someone was a good test-taker doesn't mean they're going to be a Rockstar. Intelligence and book smarts are useful, but cognitive ability—the ability to learn, make decisions, and adjust one's approach based on new information—is far more valuable. After going back to study the correlation, even Google no longer sets a minimum GPA for all employees, a practice it once swore by.

BRAINTEASERS

If you're still asking brainteaser questions, stop. Things like, "Why is a manhole cover round?" or "How many birdcages are there in New York City?" will not help you figure out who to hire. Google was famous for these questions early on; they've banned them, too.

GUT FEEL

Meeting a candidate for lunch and asking, "So tell me about yourself," will not reveal whether they are a Rockstar. You may leave the interview with a comforting gut feel, but the gut misleads.

PREDICTORS OF SUCCESS

Now you know some of the traits that are not predictive of success. So, let's look at those that are.

TEST DRIVE

According to a 1998 study by Schmidt and Hunter, the single best predictor of success is the Test Drive. It needs to be a mandatory part of your hiring process. We'll delve into the Test Drive later, but, in the meantime, think of it as a dry run with the candidate to see how they perform in the real world. They take a bit of time, so you won't be able to put all candidates through one. So, I use the interview process to determine whom I'd like to invest that time with.

STRUCTURED INTERVIEW

If you ask the same questions in the same order to each candidate, you'll be able do two things: 1. follow the trend line of a candidate in his career, and 2. assess the candidates against each other. The key is to be methodical and consistent. This can be boring and monotonous for the interviewer, but it's not about keeping yourself entertained; it's about hiring the best person. When I observed my client's questions with candidates, they were random. She hopped around from job to job; there was no structure.

This made it impossible to tell if the candidate's growth and track record was accelerating, decelerating, or stuck. In addition, she couldn't compare and contrast across candidates because she asked different questions of each one. I confess. I sometimes bore myself to tears during interviews, asking the same carefully worded questions over and over and over. But by doing so, I can assess a candidate's trendline (I think of it as analogous to a stock chart). I can compare him to other candidates. And over time, I develop a better base of interviewing knowledge because I'm asking the same questions of everyone.

COGNITIVE ABILITY

This is so much more valuable than raw intellect or IQ. Can the candidate ask questions, consume information, and adjust their approach accordingly? Are they open-minded enough to take information that conflicts with their pre-existing mindset? Can they separate the signal from the noise? These characteristics aren't easy to assess, but they're vital in today's ever-changing business environment. A head of marketing, for example, can't know every single thing about every single marketing tactic. But if she has a high cognitive ability, she will know what questions to ask, where to get the answers, how to understand the data, and adapt her approach.

DNA

We devoted an entire chapter to DNA earlier because without a DNA match, the individual will be unable to succeed within your enterprise. Are the candidate's ingrained characteristics a fit with the culture, the manager, and the team? No matter how good the candidate is, if they don't work well with the hiring manager, the body's going to reject the organ.

Some studies reveal that this accounts for nearly half of a candidate's success in the organization.

COMPETENCIES

Of course, the interview will separate candidates who possess the essential characteristics needed for success in the role from those who don't.

STRONG BACKDOOR REFERENCES

These are references that I've found on my own, rather than people the candidate provided as references. We'll discuss reference checking later on.

INTERVIEWING PITFALLS

I recently added up the interviews I've conducted over the years. I'm not proud to admit that it's over 10,000. I'm sure this doesn't make me the most exciting guy at cocktail parties. But you can benefit from this, as well as the countless mistakes I've seen my clients and staff make over the years. Here are blunders that hiring managers make during interviews:

BEING UNPREPARED

Many interviewers don't prepare ahead of time, which is

a huge mistake. Often, when I observe an interview, my client hasn't even glanced at the résumé before walking in the room. That's unfortunate because you want to pay attention to the markers we outlined earlier—career movement, gaps in employment, quantified achievements, and the like. I make notes on the résumé ahead of time about questions I want to ask. What do I really need to drill into? The preparation doesn't take long, but it makes all the difference versus doing it on the fly.

STARTING AT THE BEGINNING

If you're like most executives, you've been told to start at the beginning of the candidate's story—perhaps when they were accepted to college or their first job. In a perfect world, I would agree with this wholeheartedly. I want to understand the entirety of their professional career. Unfortunately, I've learned that this isn't always possible because the interview becomes a race against the clock.

If the candidate seated before me is forty years old, he and/ or I simply may not have time for that. Instead, I focus first on the past ten years of experience (I identify before the interview precisely where I want to start). I tell the candidate that I may want to circle back to their earlier career but for now we're going to start with such-and-such role. If they haven't impressed me with their career trajectory over the past ten years, then the prior ten isn't going to make the difference. Of course, if the candidate is only twenty-five years old, we'll start at the beginning.

OVERRELIANCE ON THE INTERVIEW

It's a common mistake to assume a great interviewee will be a great employee. I've hired people who gave mediocre interviews and turned out to be my best employees. On the other hand, some people who gave great interviews were let go after three months. This is especially common with sales candidates, many of whom are great talkers. Turns out there's not a strong correlation between great interviewers and great employees, so I've learned to use the interview as one input into the hiring decision as opposed to the end-all, be-all factor.

CONFIRMATION BIAS

It's human nature. We tend to prefer people like ourselves and hire people like ourselves. This is the danger of bias. As a result, we tend to form a quick opinion about people and then spend the remaining time looking for data that confirms our original hypothesis. Thus, we hire people who look, talk, and act like we do. We're drawn toward people who went to the same school or belong to the same clubs.

When you first meet a candidate, you'll likely decide whether you like them or not in the first twenty seconds. The brain does this automatically as a survival mechanism. Confirmation bias leads to the information we seek in order to reinforce the decision we've already made, even a snap decision. In other words, you quickly decide "She's a winner" or "He'd make a lousy sales rep," then you subconsciously spend the remainder of the interview seeking information to reinforce your original hypothesis.

Rather than fight that gut instinct, I listen to it and use it to my advantage. After twenty seconds, I'll ask my brain what its initial feeling is. It tells me, yet I will assume that it's wrong. In fact, I'll spend the next hour seeking information to overturn my original conclusion. It keeps me sharp and makes the laborious process of interviewing a whole lot more interesting. I think of it like a detective TV show—you know the one with twists and turns, and the murderer isn't who you thought it would be, and the guilty-faced person was nothing more than a bystander. Often, by the end of the interview, I've changed my mind. It happens in a significant percentage of my interviews, and I've been doing this for twenty-five years. Candidates surprise me; they'll surprise you, too, (in both directions) if you just give them the chance.

OVERRELIANCE ON THE RÉSUMÉ

Another mistake is treating the résumé as factual. On many occasions, there are things a candidate didn't include on the résumé that I'll uncover, which dissuade me from hiring the person. I also dig for crucial data omitted from the document that makes the individual particularly well-suited for the role. Remember, the résumé is simply a sales brochure, regardless of how sexy their chosen font.

NO SCORECARD

A lack of clarity about the position's needs is a fatal flaw. Understand up front what you're looking for, so that you know if you find it during the interview. If you don't have a Scorecard, there's no way to gauge the interview, and if that's the case, you're wasting a lot of people's time, including your own. I keep my Scorecard right in front of me as I interview. It's a constant reminder of what I'm hunting for. Also, it's very easy to forget which candidate is which, who did what, and what impression they made on me. Additionally, how do I compare my observations with the other interviewers if I haven't promptly captured my impressions? Don't leave this to chance or to a quick text message. This decision is far too important.

TOO FEW OR TOO MANY INTERVIEWS

I've had clients make offers based on one interview. And I've had others put candidates through nearly twenty (yes, decisions took forever because you can't get twenty people to agree on anything). I knew the answer had to be in between, and finally there's proof. According to a study by Google of its own recruiting history, four interviews is the optimal number. Four interviews reveal substantially more information than three, while a fifth adds barely any new value. Only one interviewer is necessary at a time. You'll get four different perspectives on each candidate. But don't have each ask the same questions—get additional information to make a well-informed decision. More on this shortly.

TOO CHATTY

Another mistake is for the interviewer to speak more than 20 percent of the time. The candidate should be doing most of the talking. Once you choose candidates to move forward in the process, of course, you'll invest time selling your company and the role. But in the initial interview, save your talking for the beginning and the end.

BEING IMPRESSED BY TITLES AND EMPLOYERS

Just because a candidate has worked at Facebook, Microsoft, or Apple doesn't mean they're a Rockstar. Yes, there's a good chance, but we're trying to remove chance from your recruiting process. The same applies to titles. Job titles don't represent the person's capacity, seniority, or scope of responsibility. A vice president at one company is not a vice president at another. Instead, focus on accomplishments and what the candidate has learned along the way.

WRONG INTERVIEW LOCATION

Interviews should take place in an office or conference room, or a hotel lobby if you're in from out of town. It shouldn't be over a meal or at a coffee shop; while I like to observe their table manners, those places are too loud and busy. If you can't meet in person, FaceTime or Skype video will suffice. They reveal far more than phone, since 90 percent of communication is non-verbal.

TYPES OF INTERVIEWS

Three types of interviews are part of a winning recruitment process: phone screen, career deep dive, and DNA match.

PHONE SCREEN

The phone screen is a fifteen- to twenty-minute phone call. The goal is simple: Do I want to advance this person to the next stage of the process, during which I'll invest a substantial amount of time? Out of the twenty people who make it this far, I will typically advance five. This round is an efficient way to filter out candidates who appear to be a high-risk hire, based on the competencies (or lack thereof).

There is a rhyme and reason to everything I do in the call, so here are the steps chronologically.

INTRODUCTION

I begin the call with a brief introduction of who I am and a short description of the company and the vacancy we're filling.

If they haven't applied, I explain humbly, "I'm not here to sell you anything. We are doing some fantastic things. It's a really exciting time for the business. The role may or may not be of interest to you and if not that's totally fine. It may be a great fit for someone you know, and I welcome your thoughts on that. If it's of interest to you, I'm happy to have that discussion as well."

This reduces the pressure of the call, just as a great sales professional does during a sales call.

JUST THE FIRST DATE

The second thing I say is that I don't need an answer at the end of the call. Let them know there's no pressure. They can think about whether they'd like to have another conversation, and if so, we'll find time to do that around their schedule.

You are looking for enough information in these twenty minutes to decide if you want to invest another two hours with this person. I consider it a first date.

I try to get them talking a bit about themselves, during which

I can assess communications, the scope of their current role, and areas of dissatisfaction. To do that, I say, "I've taken a look at your LinkedIn profile and it's impressive. Unfortunately, they're not always up to date. Perhaps you could take sixty seconds and give me a sense of what you're working on these days." The vast majority of people won't hesitate to provide a synopsis of their company and role. This tells me whether I've found a potential candidate, or someone who is clearly too junior or senior for the role.

During the call, I'm assessing their competencies; I want to substantiate their résumé or LinkedIn profile. I'm also taking copious notes to use the information in future interviews and for the purpose of selling later. I find out in what ways they may be dissatisfied with their current situation (too long a commute, under-market compensation, a micro-managing boss, and the like). And I write that down, as it'll come in handy later when I can remind them of greener pastures. I also ask if there's anything they would change about their current role. I'm gauging their satisfaction level. I write down their answers, so I can use that information later to persuade them to join my organization. It will form the basis of how I sell them on the position.

This call is short, so I focus on their current role and, if it's a brief tenure, the one before it. This isn't a full career history; there's no time for that. I ask about each of the last two jobs: What is your single biggest accomplishment? How did you achieve it? What problems did you have to overcome? I'm seeking evidence of any quantifiable, demonstrable results that would be correlative to the competencies required in the role I'm looking to fill. If their "biggest accomplishments" leave me underwhelmed, the person's probably not right for the job.

These questions will tell me what they consider an accomplishment and shine some light on their cognitive ability. I'll also get a sense of their passion, grit, and persistence.

NON-COMPETE

If the candidate happens to be from within the industry, I take a moment to ask them if they're bound by any non-compete agreement with their employer (or, if they recently left the employer, whether there's one still in effect—often they're one or two years in duration). Why? Because I've fallen in love with far too many candidates only to find out late in the game that they were un-hirable (or at least not without a lawsuit). So, ask early. The answer may surprise you.

REFERENCES

While it may be premature, I explain that I'd like to understand who—if we get to an endpoint in the process—their references would be. I focus on the past three to five employers, asking who would be the reference for each situation. If they can't provide a reference for virtually every role they've held for the past ten years—or if most of those references aren't their direct managers—it raises at least a yellow flag. It doesn't necessarily mean the person isn't a Rockstar, but I'm not in the business of taking risks. If they give me a reference that isn't a manager, I try to understand why.

Often, hiring managers invest a lot of time in a candidate only to find out toward the end of the process that the person doesn't have solid references. At that point, most people find it difficult to let the person go, so they hire them anyway, only to find out later there was a good reason they didn't have references. Most Rockstars are able to get nearly every past manager on the phone and that person will say, "If you don't hire this person, you're a bozo. Best employee I ever had." So, I've learned to move this question from the end of the hiring process to the beginning. This one step alone will save you hours and hours of pointless interviews.

ANSWER THEIR BURNING QUESTIONS

During the phone screen, I give the individual five minutes to ask questions and learn about our business. I use everything they say as a marker of their motivations, passions, intelligence, and preparation. Their questions help me understand what's important to them, their reasoning skills, and whether they've done any research.

Often, I can tell their interest level from their questions. Rockstars might ask about our biggest challenges or where I think we'll be in a couple of years. They might ask about the most compelling or interesting aspect of this role and whether it will offer a challenge. They'll probably want to know if it will allow them to have ownership over something. If a candidate asks me about hours, vacation policy, or travel, that's a yellow flag. It sends the message that they're more interested in maximizing their free time than anything else.

COMPENSATION

It's a potentially huge waste of time to not discuss money early on. I've found that when I'm talking to someone who makes far less than the role I'm hiring for, they're typically too light for the position. Similarly, I don't want to waste time with candidates who are unlikely to take this position because they already earn more.

Years ago, compensation was often not at parity. In other words, I often found candidates who were dramatically underpaid or overpaid. With the advent of the Internet and countless compensation websites and studies, that range has narrowed. Just as with product pricing, compensation has become far more transparent and consistent.

I have our budget clearly established in my mind before I even ask the question. I'm typically seeking someone for whom this job would represent a 25 percent increase in compensation (salary, equity, bonuses, etc.). If my budget for this role is $100,000, for example, I'll ideally find someone who's currently earning $80,000.

I almost never pursue people for whom the compensation that I can afford would represent a reduction for them, unless it's also accompanied by equity participation in the company that could prove to be meaningful. Why? I've learned that few people—despite what they might say in the first interview—will accept a decrease. I'll invest a lot of time and they'll turn me down because they decide they can't or won't take the pay cut. In fact, I rarely invest time with candidates for whom this role doesn't represent at least a 10 percent increase. For the same reason, I've learned that few Rockstars make a move without having a compelling reason to do so. Time and again, 25 percent has been that number for me.

A good number of clients tell me that I'm overpaying or asking them to overpay—that they want to pay $85,000 to a candidate who's currently earning $80,000. Rockstar candidates simply don't move for a lateral or marginal increase.

Ask about current compensation toward the end of the phone call after you've built some rapport. I say: "Before we wrap up, would it be okay if we talked about compensation for a moment?" Invariably, they say yes—candidates don't want to waste their time either. Then I say: "Great. How is your compensation currently structured in terms of fixed versus variable versus equity? What is the total scope of it?" Then I'm silent. About 70 percent of the time, they provide the numbers. The rest provide an outline of the mix, but not the actual numbers. A simple follow-up question takes care of that: "And what was the total last year?"

Whatever their answer, be sure to understand their cash versus long-term equity compensation. You want to write down their salary, their bonus, and their equity.

I rarely provide them with the compensation package I have in mind, but I'll reassure them and let them know we're in the same range. I want them to know they're not wasting their time. Conversely, I will tell them if our budget is nowhere close to what they currently earn. Sometimes, I follow up with a question asking them to reflect on their salary. "How does where you are compare to where you'd like to be?" I'll ask. The way they answer gives me some context clues as to what will be required to entice them to make a move.

Overall, this provides invaluable information that can save you a ton of time later. I've fallen in love with countless candidates only to discover later that they were out of my range. Don't make this mistake.

ASK FOR OTHER CANDIDATES

If the phone screen conversation reveals that this isn't a fit, I shift into sourcing mode. I ask them to think about who they know who might be a great fit for the role. I tell them I'll email them tomorrow to see if any names came to mind (and I do).

The Up-and-Comer

Your hiring decision will often come down to two types of candidates: the person who's doing the same job for the same amount of money at a different company, or the person for whom this would be an upward move—more money, more responsibility, and a broader title.

In general, I find that most executives choose to hire the first type. It feels safer somehow; there's an assumption that the person will hit the ground running. That the individual is a heavyweight and there's some ego associated with "snagging" a sitting VP of marketing for our VP of marketing role. That logic makes sense, but ask yourself: Why would a Rockstar make a lateral move like this? On occasion, there are good reasons—an intolerable commute, financial troubles for the company, a title that isn't accompanied by a broad amount of responsibility, a micromanaging boss.

But more often than not, the lateral candidate is not the best choice.

Instead, I look for the up-and-comer. When I start a search for a VP of marketing, for example, I look first for Rockstar directors and senior directors of marketing. I look for them because this job will get their attention; this would be an upward move, and that's going to be exciting for them. I want someone who's going to be excited to be on my team. They have something to prove—remember the old Avis Rental Car adage, "Number two tries harder."

SET EXPECTATIONS

To wrap up the call, I share next steps with the candidate. I tell them I'm having many of these short discussions over the next week or two, and that I will have some feedback on where things stand after that. I try to provide them an actual date if I can. I set appropriate expectations and tell them that the next step would be to meet in person (or by video). I also ask them to think about their interest level and tell them to email or call with their questions.

Even if this candidate has blown me away, I resist promising the next step of an in-person meeting during this phone call. I don't give them the nod to advance to the next step, because I don't know what I'll find with my other nineteen calls. Remember, batch process so that you can compare and contrast.

I compare only once I've completed the batch. Twenty conversations typically result in five people worthy of substantial time investment. When in doubt, throw them out. You may be throwing away a Rockstar, but you must decide how to spend your precious time. You have five chips and you need to place your bets wisely.

After ending the call, I send the candidate a short email, something to restate my interest, often a short video or recent news release about the company.

> Congratulations! We started with 150, picked the twenty to invest time with, and now have it to a group of approximately five to meet in person. To get them to the table, educate them on the role, the company, and the market. Don't just take the first five that are willing to come regardless. Recruiting involves salesmanship—not just picking from the hand-raisers. And if you're lousy at selling—be honest with yourself—have the best person in your organization execute this step.

It's time to get those five in for meetings. And speaking of time, this is a great opportunity to remind you that—since you committed up front in this book to investing 30 percent to 50 percent of your time on your talent—getting the meetings in the books shouldn't take three weeks. This is a priority—your biggest priority. So, act like it. Bear in mind that currently engaged Rockstars may need to meet evenings or weekends. I work around their schedule, and I never regret it. They're my first customer. Surprisingly, some of my clients will keep a candidate waiting for a month. In the war for talent, it doesn't work that way.

There are two types of in-person interviews: the career deep dive and the DNA match. The former examines competency qualifications by exploring the candidate's career; the latter attempts to identify a personality fit, or lack thereof. A total of four interviews are conducted with each candidate, preferably during the same visit: one deep dive and three DNA match interviews, each by a different interviewer. All five of your candidates should be put through the half-day sessions in the same manner, and from them, you'll select one (or preferably two) to advance to the next step, which is a Test Drive.

CAREER DEEP DIVE

This is the big one: the extensive career review. Don't leave it to chance. Don't wing it. There is an optimal structure to the interview and, again, we'll step through it in order.

The hiring manager himself or herself should conduct the deep dive. If it's important enough to fill this vacancy, it's important enough to invest this time with five semi-finalists. To be clear, HR, talent, and people organizations add immense value to the recruitment process, particularly in assessing DNA match. Yet, only the hiring manager knows the job needs inside out; the subtleties of what's comparable, leverageable experience and what's not.

This means being prepared before ever setting foot into the room. Review the résumé ahead of time, note any questions you want to ask; be sure to note gaps in employment. You'll ask the same questions for each position, so that you can track the trajectory of their career and easily compare them to other candidates. The outcome of the interview will be a score on the agreed-upon Scorecard. And that is based in part upon the trajectory of their career. Is it heading up, down, or is it flat? By asking the same questions of each role, we can determine a pattern.

Allow an hour and a half to two hours for the interview, depending on the person's number of years of experience (the more senior, the more time), and the profile of the job.

FIRST IMPRESSIONS

We talked about confirmation bias earlier. It's okay to form your initial hypothesis about the candidate, write it down in your notes, and then spend the rest of the interview trying to overturn that hypothesis.

LAST THINGS FIRST

After I introduce myself and refresh the candidate on the scope of the opportunity, I let them ask questions first, rather than at the end of the meeting. I've always hated the cliché "last few minutes for your questions." Putting it first, right up front, has a host of advantages. The candidate has hopefully done some research at this point and should be somewhat prepared to ask questions. The questions they ask are indicative of their level of interest, engagement, and preparation—or not.

Their questions speak volumes—are they already sold, or do I have a lot of convincing to do? Those questions will also shine light on their cognitive ability. Finally, it helps put them at ease. I want to interview the authentic person, not the nervous candidate. Giving them a few minutes to cover at least their burning questions gives them time to get comfortable and turn a high-pressure interview into a relaxed conversation.

We spend fifteen minutes or so on their questions, and then I take over. I say, "I'm glad we got through some of your questions. And it won't be your last chance to ask. Now, I'd love to learn more about your background and experience. I don't have any trick questions. I'm not here to stump you. I just want to understand the context and scope of each role over the past ten years." I'll ask the same questions for each role.

I spend about twenty minutes on each position they've held, starting ten years ago and working my way to the present. As much as I dislike it, I take notes using pen and paper; a laptop or tablet placed between me and the candidate negatively affects the dynamic. I type far faster than I handwrite, but I find that the device just creates a barrier.

THE QUESTIONS

Here are the questions that I ask each candidate of each role. It's important to stick to the program and conduct the interviews the same way each time, so that you can measure them against each other accurately.

WHAT WERE THE START AND END DATE OF THE ROLE?

This is important because dates on résumés are often incorrect or out of date. Sometimes, they're misleading. If someone joined a company in December and left after six weeks, that might read as two years of employment if the résumé only lists the dates by year. In fact, I largely discount roles that were shorter than twenty-four months in duration. In my career, both as an executive and as a recruiter, I've learned that it takes two years to learn a business, lay out a plan, execute that plan, see the results, and adjust accordingly.

In some roles, this can be twelve months, but particularly

for mid-level to senior roles, it's two years. You need to eat your own cooking, to live with the decisions you made in the business last year. So, six weeks, six months, even twelve months just do not tell me much. Were you good or were you lucky? I have no way of knowing. Since I'm trying to de-risk the hire, I largely discount short-tenure roles.

WHY DID YOU CHOOSE TO JOIN THE COMPANY?

This helps me understand their decision-making process, their passions, and their true motivators.

WHAT WAS THE CHARTER OF THE ROLE?

This tells me why they were hired and what they were asked to do in the role.

WHAT DID YOU INHERIT?

I want to know if it was a turnaround situation or if they inherited a winning hand, a Rockstar team, etc. What was the size of their team, their budget, and/or resources they began with?

WHAT WAS THE ORGANIZATIONAL CONTEXT?

I need to understand how they fit in. Titles are often misleading. So, who were their peers? Their manager? Their team? How did that group fit in with the broader context of the company? Did they lead a geography or a product or a team? Was it an individual contributor role?

WHAT WERE YOUR QUANTIFIABLE ACCOMPLISHMENTS IN THIS ROLE?

I'm looking for candidates who are data-driven and eager to tell me about their accomplishments. They leave a mark. You know they were there. That's where we're more likely to find Rockstars.

HOW DID YOU ACHIEVE THOSE RESULTS?

The killer question that many interviewers don't ask is "How?" It's great that they achieved results, but we need to know *how*. This is where the story will start to either make sense or fall apart. I need to know if they were lucky or talented. Were they a solo hero, or did they lead a team effort? Was there a plan, or was it chaotic? I'm not interrogating them or suggesting that I don't believe them. I'm simply trying to understand how they did what they did. And I'll dig for details: "How?" "How?" "How?" I sound like an owl, but after a few minutes, I learn if it was the real thing or if the story begins to unravel.

For example, consider Sales Rep A and Sales Rep B. Their résumés are similar. Both made Presidents Club last year.

Sales Rep A found success because he landed one killer account that fell into his lap. In fact, the previous sales rep in the territory sourced that account. He got lucky. Sales Rep B built a pipeline and systematically pursued and prosecuted the leads. Her sales were not tied to one account. Her close-rate was exceptional. She landed twelve accounts. Who would you rather hire?

WHAT WAS YOUR BIGGEST FAILURE IN THE ROLE?

I'm looking for humility, emotional intelligence, and the capacity to learn from their mistakes. Can they identify what they might have done differently?

WHAT CHALLENGES DID YOU FACE AND HOW DID YOU OVERCOME THEM?

I'm looking for resiliency in the face of conflict and their ability to adjust their approach as situations evolve.

WHAT WAS YOUR MANAGER'S STYLE AND HOW DID YOU WORK TOGETHER?

I'm trying to assess if this candidate will enjoy and mesh with my style (or the style of the hiring manager). Does she prefer a hands-off manager? Or does she appreciate the attention to detail of a micromanager? What does she expect of a manager? Will they drive each other crazy?

WHAT DID YOU ENJOY MOST AND LEAST ABOUT THE ROLE?

This will tell me whether they're likely to enjoy the role we're discussing. It shows me what tasks they consider to be interesting, what their passions are, and things they don't enjoy doing. If they say, for example, that they hated the travel, and I know that this role may have 80 percent travel, we're setting ourselves up for failure.

HOW WAS THE COMPENSATION STRUCTURED?

We asked this same question on the phone screen, but now we're asking it for each role going back ten years. I'm looking for the trajectory of their compensation increasing over time. I don't expect them to have a perfect mastery of the numbers (although sales candidates typically do), but I do want to understand the trend, as well as the mix of fixed versus variable, and short-term versus long-term compensation. This reveals much about their risk profile.

IF WE GET TO THE REFERENCE STAGE, WHAT SHOULD I EXPECT TO HEAR WHEN I SPEAK WITH YOUR MANAGER?

A Rockstar will say, "He's going to rave about me." I'm looking for whether this candidate can get their manager on the phone to be a reference, and if they have a clear understanding of what the manager will say about them. Rockstars want me to speak with their references and they can promptly arrange the discussion. B-Players hem and haw. "I can't find him," "I lost track of her," "She left the company." Thanks to LinkedIn, I can track down virtually anyone. I assure the candidate that I can—and will—track down their former manager, so I'd prefer to hear it from them first. At this point, candidates spill their guts.

WHY DID YOU CHOOSE TO MOVE ON FROM THIS ROLE?

I ask the question this way to lower their guard. They may say, "Well, I didn't choose to move on. They asked me to leave." Were they terminated? Did they fail? Did they get a promotion and move on? Were they recruited to work elsewhere? I don't dismiss a candidate who was terminated—as long as I can validate in referencing that it wasn't for an ethics violation. Some of the best Rockstars joined a company in which they didn't fit (i.e., lousy recruiting) and were shown the door. But if it's more than one for each ten years of work history, I dig for explanations.

I know there's a lot here, but when you're thorough and consistent, you'll find that the stories of a Rockstar remain intact, while those of wannabes just fall apart. To save you time, I've created a template that you can print out and use during interviews. Grab it free at www.RecruitRockstars.com/Bonus

TIME ALLOCATION

Again, ask these questions for each of the candidate's roles over the last ten years. And write down the answers. I know that sounds silly, but if you're going to invest 30 to 50 percent of your time scouting talent, you're going to thank yourself for doing so. Aim to interview all five candidates within a one-week period. This will help you keep them straight in your mind. It also keeps the process moving along. But this is hard work, so don't do more than two in a day. Schedule at least an hour and a half (twenty minutes per role x four roles = eighty minutes).

SCORECARD TIME

After you've escorted the candidate out, complete your Scorecard within thirty minutes. Review your notes and rate the candidate from 1 to 10 on the competencies you previously determined were essential for success in the role. If someone is an 8, 9, or 10, they're a great candidate. By the definition stated earlier, only 5 percent of people are Rockstars—those are the ones receiving 8s, 9s, and 10s on the Scorecard. So, most of your candidates are likely 5s, 6s, and 7s. Anything below an 8, I simply will not hire. The more you interview, the more comfortable you'll become at scoring.

THE DNA MATCH

Okay, we've assessed and probed their work history, their

accomplishments, their *referenceability*. If your company is like most, you'll now have the candidate meet with three or five or eighteen more interviewers who essentially ask the same questions. What a lost opportunity! We've already covered the work history, and nobody is more qualified than the hiring manager to assess that degree of fit. But we're not done.

The next three interviews (for a total of four) are all about the candidate's DNA. You're looking to assess if they will be a good match for your company. Find three employees who are outstanding representatives of your company's DNA to conduct the interviews for all five candidates. The hiring manager should not conduct any of these, assuming they did the career exploration interview. You're looking for three perspectives, gleaned from three different interviewers. And it must be the same interviewers for all five candidates, so that they can compare apples to apples. Having some interviewers meet only some of the candidates defeats the intention of a fact-based process.'

Each DNA interview should last approximately one hour. As before, give the candidate a chance to ask questions for the first five to ten minutes and then tell them you'd like to talk about some examples from their life. There are fewer questions in these interviews; you're just asking them over and over to get past the rehearsed examples to the authentic individual.

Each interviewer will focus on one or two DNA characteristics that you've decided are intrinsic to your organization, like resilience, optimism, or creativity. We're looking for anecdotal evidence of their DNA traits.

THE QUESTIONS TO ASK

TELL ME ABOUT A TIME WHEN YOU HAD TO EXHIBIT... (THE DNA CHARACTERISTIC THAT THE INTERVIEWER IS FOCUSING ON)

After they answer, ask for two or three more examples. If the candidate can give you credible, engaging examples that are consistent with your definition of that characteristic, chances are good that they share your DNA and will be a good fit at your company. This person may have bombed the career exploration interview, however; in that case, try to find him a different spot in the organization because it's difficult to find someone who shares your DNA.

TELL ME ABOUT YOUR FAVORITE JOB EVER
TELL ME ABOUT YOUR LEAST FAVORITE JOB EVER

Look for whether what they describe is consistent with the job you're looking to fill. If they tell you, for example, that they disliked a job because it lacked variety, and I happen to be looking for the DNA of creativity, that's a promising sign.

TELL ME ABOUT YOUR BEST BOSS EVER
TELL ME ABOUT YOUR WORST MANAGER EVER

Again, I'm looking for consistency between their preferences and the manager for this role.

TELL ME ABOUT THE WORK ENVIRONMENT YOU THRIVED IN MOST
TELL ME ABOUT THE WORK ENVIRONMENT YOU FOUND THE MOST DIFFICULT

Here, I'm also looking for whether it's consistent with our environment. The idea, again, is to drill and keep on drilling to get past the rehearsed answers and find authentic ones.

Each interviewer completes their Scorecard within thirty minutes, rating the candidate and jotting down any notes to debrief with the rest of the interview team.

ASSESSING THE CANDIDATES

Within twenty-four hours of all five candidates completing all four interviews, gather as an interview team. It's best to do this in person, but video will suffice. Debate, discuss, argue, and go into the fine points. Don't accept statements such as, "I really like this guy." You're only focusing on things that are measurable and predictive.

Your job is to narrow the five candidates down to a first

choice and a second choice. If only one has the requisite competencies and DNA, that's fine. Don't settle for number two just to have a second choice. If the scores are such that one of your candidates is a 9 and the other is a 7.5, keep the 7.5 in the running because you may not land the 9. If one is a 9 and the other is a 4, only one advances in the process.

The team should also talk about any concerns they want to dig into, plus begin discussing how to convince their top choice to join the organization.

REMEMBER THE CANDIDATE EXPERIENCE

When highly structured, the interview process can be far more useful in predicting the success of a candidate. However, you can't simply force candidates through the process. It takes some handling and fine-tuning. So, consider it from the candidate's perspective.

The experience that candidates have at your company matters—even the candidates who don't receive the offer (which will be the vast majority). Their experience during the interview is the first and only representation they'll have of your company. You'll damage your employer brand with a bad candidate experience, just as you damage your consumer brand with a bad customer experience. It doesn't take much. And you'll read about it on Glassdoor.

After the interview team has met, the hiring manager or an HR representative should provide prompt, direct feedback to the candidates. Feedback should include what you saw that makes them a great fit and concerns you'd like to discuss further.

Candidate experience also includes how compelling the Job Invitation was, how easy it was to apply, and whether they were asked the same questions in multiple interviews. Did the interviewers begin the interview on time? Did someone offer the candidate coffee or water? Were they warmly welcomed?

Pay attention to all the touchpoints—from the Job Invitation to the offer letter to the welcome basket and everything in between. Make sure that every interaction is a first-class experience for candidates. Rockstars deserve and expect that, and it will help you dramatically when it's time to get the "Yes."

In this chapter, we talked about predictors of success, interviewing mistakes, the three types of interviews, candidate assessment, and candidate experience.

In the next chapter, we'll talk about the Test Drive, which is the single most predictive tool you have for assessing candidates.

CHAPTER 6

TAKE CANDIDATES ON A TEST DRIVE

IIIIIIIIIIIIIIIIIII

I'm going to let you in on a little secret.

Nine out of ten hiring managers skip the most predictive component of the entire recruiting process. That's right. The one thing that is most likely to make the difference between a great hire and a bad hire—completely bypassed. What is it?

The Test Drive. A real-world simulation that mirrors the actual work tasks that the candidate will be asked to accomplish if they get the nod. Some call it the job audition or the dry run, but whatever it's called, it simply must be part of your process. If you take away nothing else from this book, add this step and you'll spare yourself a good number of mis-hires.

Thirty years ago, a landmark study found that the Test Drive is the single best tool we can use when assessing candidates. It's more accurate than interviews, reference checks, intelligence tests, education, or any other element. So, I insist upon it for every role at every level—from office manager to CEO. It's so illuminating, yet just 9 percent of companies use it consistently. We can't implement it at the beginning of the process, because it's too time-consuming to execute it with twenty candidates, or even five.

Yet, the Test Drive allows you to see finalist candidates in action, actually performing work similar to what they'd be doing in the position. Even if you follow everything we've discussed throughout the rest of the interview process, there's still a chance you'll make a hiring mistake—because answering questions in the safe confines of an austere conference room is far different than actually doing the work.

That said, don't bypass the interview phase, because it is a necessity. It provides information about competencies and DNA. Those are predictive of whether the candidate will thrive in your environment once they prove themselves capable during the Test Drive.

By adding the Test Drive to your process, you'll increase your hiring accuracy from 50 or 60 percent to 70 or 80 percent. That's huge. This step has changed my mind time and again about particular candidates—in both directions. Candidates who perform admirably during interviews sometimes fall apart during the Test Drives. And others—introverts or those demonstrating unrefined social skills during interviews— have blown me (and my clients) away.

Candidates—especially Rockstars—love the Test Drive, too, because it allows them to see the company and the hiring manager in action. It's akin to dating before marriage. It also provides a forum for Rockstars to demonstrate their best handiwork.

Because they're used so rarely, the Test Drive also serves to differentiate your company as being creative and compelling. It makes the statement, "We take recruiting seriously here." The exercise helps candidates engage more deeply with your company and increases the likelihood that they'll say, "Yes," if given an offer. They've invested more time, hopefully enjoyed the process, and will have had the opportunity to see what the work will be like. The result is fewer surprises for both parties.

You may be skeptical about the value of the Test Drive. Sounds like a lot of work? Don't just take my word for it. Here's the experience of a true believer, someone who's used this method for years. Mary Beth Wynn is Senior Vice

President of People at Chicago-based Jellyvision. Here's what she has to say:

> Our audition process originated with hiring for our Writer role. We ask candidates to provide some custom writing samples, because our tone is so unique. That has expanded so that having an audition for every role in the company is an important part of our hiring process. Auditions let us focus less on where you went to school or how many years of experience you've got—and let us see more of what your actual work product is like.

> If we don't see a fit during the initial interview, we don't advance to an audition because we don't want to ask anyone to invest that kind of time and effort if we don't think there's going to be a fit. With some candidates, I've been excited after speaking with them, and then they bomb the audition. But there definitely have been candidates who weren't my favorite going into the audition phase, who submitted an audition that showed us more of what they can do than how they presented in the first interview. So, it's a really good check against what we're seeing in initial interviews.

> One of our best auditions is in Sales, for our Business Development Representative roles. They are our appointment setters, and are on the phone all day. So, we prepare some personas and tell them, "These are your potential targets,"

and have them make a series of calls over a half-hour. We are looking to see that they've researched the persona and have an approach to how they're going to try to speak with that person based on the information we've given them. We throw them some curveballs to see how they react. And we do a little coaching. We have them make a call, and then we say "Hey, 'this' was great, we'd like to see you do more of 'this,'" and see if they can incorporate that coaching into the additional calls. It really is an actual phone call. They call the conference room, where we've got a group of people role-playing the potential clients.

We're looking to see things like: Are they improving over the course of the calls? How do they react to curveballs? Do they take the coaching well? We're also looking to see if they are "persistent in a lovely way." Some of the personas are happy to hear from you. Sometimes you get someone who is trying to get off the phone and is really negative. So, we try to vary the personas so that when they get someone on the phone who is saying "No, no, I don't think this is for me," we want to see if they can be persistent in a way that is kind, and has a Jellyvision delightful spin to it.

So, what does the Test Drive look like in action? It can be two hours, half a day, or two days. It's a relatively short-term, real-world scenario. You'll observe the candidate as they perform crucial tasks. Provide data and a timeframe, and see how they use logic and reasoning skills to problem-solve. You'll see how they follow instructions, or when they think out of the box, delivering something beyond your expectations. You'll get a glimpse into how they think by the questions they ask. It's telling for a host of reasons.

No one buys a car without a Test Drive, right? You'll see it in the showroom (the résumé); ask the car salesperson questions (the interview) and then, you'll take it out for a spin. You've already determined it fits your budget and has the features you want. But only on the wide-open road can you gauge the acceleration, the handling, and the performance. You truly see what it can do. That's what Test Drives accomplish with your candidates. And the results will surprise you, too.

To be clear, I'm not referring to "job shadowing," during which an employer invites a finalist candidate to spend time on a ride-along with a sales rep in the field or watch a team do its work. That's useful for observation and for cementing a hesitant candidate. They aren't here to observe how it's done; they're here to *do*. This should be arguably the best work you'll ever see. If there are typos or mathematical errors or logical flaws, that's a huge red flag. If they clash or aggravate your team during their first assignment, that's not a good sign either.

The exercise itself, including the length and format, will vary by role. For individual performance roles, a two-day homework assignment may make sense: create a presentation of this, show us how you'd code that, etc. For leadership and executive roles, I prefer a half-day session including key players whom the person will work with on the job. You'll go through a mini-exercise in which you observe how they perform in a real-world situation. How do they think, lead, and communicate? Are they rigid or open to new ideas? Are they authoritative or demure?

Let's take a real-life example with an opening for a product manager. You might tell the finalist candidate about a product that you launched last year but isn't selling well in the market. Ask them to develop a game plan. Should we kill the product, or continue with it? Does it need to be changed? How and why?

You're not looking for a specific answer, as much as their reasoning and interaction with others in pursuit of the best solution. You might have them join with someone from sales, finance, and marketing. Note whether they lead the discussion or take a passive approach in the discussion. Do they lead and inspire others? Do they imagine the possibilities, and create viable tactics to achieve them? Or do they give off a negative vibe? Do they demonstrate the competencies for the role? Are they data-driven? Are they creative in their problem-solving?

Another type of exercise can be longer, and involves the

candidate analyzing information or creating something. This is appropriate for more individual contributor roles. Let's use a software developer as an example. You could create an assignment for them to complete at home. You might ask them to write a piece of code or explain how they would write it. Give them a day or two, perhaps a week, depending on the project.

Be consistent: Provide the same exact assignment to each of your final candidates for the same role. Write out the assignment; include time constraints, expectations of the deliverable, and the tools the candidate is permitted to use (Google, a friend, a book). Is there any background information about the company that you'll need to provide?

I haven't found a role yet for which I can't design a Test Drive. Be mindful of whether the role is primarily team-based or an individual function, then design the Test Drive appropriately.

Let's look at some other examples.

SENIOR EXECUTIVES

Executive roles demand competencies in leadership, delegation, and the ability to hold people accountable. You might have a candidate attend a staff meeting to see whether they make meaningful contributions and advance the discussion. You might ask them to make a strategy presentation and answer follow-up questions. You're assessing their leadership style and how they engage with others. One of my recent clients was a Board of Directors assessing candidates for the CEO role. We had the two finalists spend one-half day each with the Board, facilitating discussions, working through strategic issues. By the end, their first-choice candidate had emerged: a Rockstar.

CHIEF FINANCIAL OFFICER

Provide your company's financial information for the past quarter and have the candidate prepare a written analysis and PowerPoint presentation, which they then present in person. Look for their insights, clarity of analysis, and ability to make assumptions. There are countless traits that are unascertainable in an interview, which emerge (or don't!) during the Test Drive.

CUSTOMER SERVICE MANAGER

Consider having a finalist for head of customer service sit in on some live calls. Have them take notes, evaluate the team, and provide feedback. Look at how they interact with the staff. Even ask your staff for feedback—did they hear any useful ideas from this person?

The Test Drive process scales nicely over time. Develop a Test Drive for each role at your company. Start with the ones you hire most often first, then build on that library. Learn what other companies do, and adapt their ideas. Your head of HR should help create these with hiring managers. They can then be re-used over time, with minor updates.

Remember that candidates usually welcome the opportunity to do the Test Drive. Rockstars love it. If you get resistance, your candidate might not be a Rockstar, or they may be hesitant to invest the time (a sign that you have more selling to do).

If necessary, consider paying your candidates for their time in taking the Test Drive. You can say, "We're not looking for free work. We're looking to ensure that there's a fit, that you can do the job as we believe you can, and we're happy to pay you for your time."

Ideally, both of your two finalist candidates pass the Test Drive, but if one doesn't, they're out, no matter how good the rest of the interview process was.

After the Test Drive, it's time to check references, which you'll use to validate everything you've heard thus far. We'll talk about that in the next chapter.

CHAPTER 7

USE REFERENCES THE RIGHT WAY

||||||||||||||||||||

I dodged the bullet. Just months before writing this book, I identified a candidate for a senior vacancy at a private equity-funded company in the business services category. The company does about $100 million in annual revenue, and this was a vital role. My client was the CEO, who retained me to help him find a new head of sales. We did a ton of research and evaluated nearly 200 candidates.

One of the candidates lives in Chicago, as I do. He did exceptionally well in the interviews and was a great match in terms of competencies. His interest level in the role was high, and he viewed it as a step forward in his career. I had a high level of confidence that I would present him to my client as a semi-finalist, and they'd have a love connection.

Since we live in the same city, I figured we must have some people in common in our networks. I got to work using LinkedIn and, sure enough, found dozens of mutual connections. In particular, two were people I know very well, and who had worked closely with this candidate for years. Early on a Thursday evening, I sent them each a text asking if I could chat with them the following day for a few minutes about a candidate I was considering. Both of them said they'd be happy to, and coincidentally asked, "By the way, who's the candidate?" I texted his name.

Within moments, they responded with virtually identical messages.

One said, "Run, don't walk, in the other direction." The other said, "I wouldn't touch him with a ten-foot pole."

I nearly spit out my Cabernet. I asked them, "What am I missing? What's the issue?" Both told me that the candidate had just been terminated for cause, due to major ethics issues. Of course, he neglected to mention this during our interviews. It turned out that he had lied, saying he wanted to find something different, that he was bored.

While not always the case, people who resign from a position before lining up their next role wave a bright yellow flag. In general, Rockstar candidates don't give up their current post until they find something they'd like to do next. In this case, both of my connections validated his bald-faced lie. Therein lies the power of backdoor references: to find out the cold hard facts about a candidate, and to validate what we've been told thus far.

Reference checking is a step that many executives skip, and they're playing with fire. It's time-consuming, a hassle to schedule, and—I'm convinced—conflicts with the egotistical pride we hold in our decision-making ability and judgment. Unfortunately, Test Drives are imperfect and interviews are even worse.

So, we simply must use references. But if you're going to do it, you might as well do it the right way to get the most out of them. I've learned the hard way to "trust but verify" every single candidate before making an offer. Remember the goal of this entire recruiting process—it's to *de-risk* the hire. Most of the time, candidates tell you their version of the truth. Whether they are purposefully deceitful or unintentionally naïve, you need to get the full story in order to make the best possible hiring decision. And sometimes, it's as blatant a lie as the one above. I saved myself a world of hurt with two quick texts.

Naturally, candidates present things in the best possible light. Sometimes, their perspective is different from their hiring manager's, though, which is why you must call the previous supervisor to hear both sides of the story. And to validate the facts you've been told through the recruiting process.

Reference checks, by the way, are only useful if they're done *prior* to making your hiring decision. Don't use them to check a box after the fact. If you're going to invest the time anyway, do so prior to deciding so that you can use the information you glean as a factor in your decision making. If you've done your job well during sourcing, interviewing, and Test Driving, references won't change your mind often—perhaps just 5 percent of the time. There shouldn't be many surprises at this late stage in the game. But on the occasion they do, you'll save yourself another bad hire and remind yourself of their value. I know it's painful to invest all that time—months often—with a candidate who seems ideally suited for the role and for your culture. And then you check references, only to find it was all an illusion. You invested that time for nothing, and you're resentful. You'll be tempted to look the other way and ignore what you heard from the references. You'll rationalize their commentary. Don't do it. When that bad hire starts to disappoint you and you're forced to part ways with them, you'll regret not heeding the references.

Equally important to verifying information, references can give you information that will help you lead and manage the person to get the most out of them. Even Rockstars need to be led, each one coached in their own unique way. I've learned to view reference checks as a shortcut that will save me time later. It's become a valuable time investment, not a hassle. Even if the references do nothing but confirm what I found in the interviews, they provide powerful ways for me to help my newly hired Rockstars excel.

All this said, reference checks are one input into the final decision. Do not allow one bad reference to dissuade you. Not everyone fits into every environment or clicks with their manager perfectly. Look for patterns. If there was one manager they didn't get along with, one company culture they didn't fit with, that might be okay. One instance doesn't make a trend. That's why it's important to check several references. I'll check as many as time allows, but always at least four.

As a bonus—or better yet, a reward for your persistence—reference checking is a great way to identify additional outstanding candidates. Rockstars know Rockstars, right? Often, the reference may be someone you want to add to your team—now, or in the future. Don't be shy: Ask about their career aspirations and current situation.

If you build a good rapport during your conversation, references will often suggest, "You also ought to talk to this guy. He would be great in that role, too."

In general, Rockstars love the fact that you're reference checking, while B- and C-Players don't. Rockstars are able to produce their references quickly and are eager for you to speak with them. I've had candidates, after our interview, unprompted, email me a list of twenty references, every person they've ever worked with. That speaks volumes about the confidence this person has in what these people are going to say. I love *referenceability*, and value it as much as what the actual references say.

Similarly, if someone makes excuses for not providing references, it raises a red flag. You'll hear excuses like, "We lost touch," or "I don't know where he is," or "She's not allowed to give references." The candidate I mentioned earlier had told me his company had a policy not to give references. Sometimes, that's true because companies fear legal recourse if the person in question doesn't get a job after a negative reference, but you'll find that Rockstars' managers will often talk to you anyway. They're almost always happy to give a great reference because, legally, there's nothing for them to fear.

If a candidate gives excuses instead of phone numbers of his former supervisors, move on. You want the least risky hire possible. If a candidate is not referenceable, you're taking on too much risk. I may be bypassing a Rockstar, but I'm more worried about allowing a B-Player onto my team. This is why it's crucial to always have a backup candidate. It's painful to spend months on this process and end up with one candidate who turns out to be *unreferenceable*. Sadly, most executives look the other way and still proceed with the hire, and that's trouble.

Throughout the interview process, keep track of every name the candidate drops. Write them down—their managers, peers, staff, customers, vendors, investors, partners, advertising agencies. When it's time to check references, ask to speak to so-and-so who the candidate mentioned he'd worked with on a project. It's fair game. Look to see who's missing from the reference list that the candidate mentioned throughout the interviews. It's telling.

If they've held ten or more roles over the course of their career but can only produce two or three managers, that tells you something. Study the ratio of managers that candidates provide and the ones they can't produce as references, and use this information to inform your decision making.

The reference check can be an invaluable tiebreaker between your final two candidates. Go into it with the mindset that you'll be willing to change your mind if you hear something troubling about one of your candidates. If you can't do that, you're just going through the motions and wasting your time.

Contact references before the offer is made. That sounds obvious, but half the time, my clients either skip it or do it after they've already extended the offer.

Want to delegate reference checking to someone else, such as your human resources team? Sorry. In my view, the hiring manager must do the reference checks, particularly since they'll obtain invaluable insights into how best to lead the new hire. And don't delegate reference checks to an outside recruiter; that is a conflict of interest. The recruiter has invested lots of time by this point and wants to get the ball across the finish line. The last thing they want to do is to uncover a problem at this point in the process. Also, they'll never care quite as much as you do. That said, I'll do the reference checks for my clients if they're too busy. But I have a twelve-month placement guarantee, so I need to get the hire right just as much as they do. Many search firms don't have a placement guarantee—or a brief one—so they'll never need to eat their own cooking.

So, who to speak with?

FRONT-DOOR REFERENCES

These are the references the candidate has provided. Ask the candidate to help you set up these meetings. Request a list of references with each one's role, relationship, email address, mobile phone, and LinkedIn profile. Then ask what you should expect to hear from the reference. Say, "I'd rather hear it from you first." This usually compels the candidate to be transparent about anything not so glossy that happened in that role. As I have the phone call with the reference, I can ask about whatever negative circumstance the candidate mentioned. A lawyer never puts a witness on the stand without knowing what they're going to say.

Just as during the interview phase, you'll want to focus on managers from the past ten years; going back into ancient history reveals little usable data. You may not be able to speak to their current manager, especially if their job search is confidential. Give them a pass on that one. You can even give them a pass on one other manager—someone they never clicked with, or a company they regret working for. But in general, they should be able to provide the majority of direct managers over the past decade. Don't take their first list at face value. If there's someone missing whom you expected to see, or want to see based on your copious interview notes, inquire.

You want to focus on direct managers because they can provide data no else can. Only a manager can tell you how your candidate performed relative to the manager's expectations, and compared to others on the team at the time. Only a manager can tell you how the candidate compares to everyone else she's ever hired. Only a manager can tell you about the difficult discussions that occurred behind closed doors.

If the candidate is just out of college and hasn't had a manager, speak with their professors, coaches, and fraternity chair. Friends, relatives, and classmates are a waste of your time.

Peers and co-workers can be useful, but primarily in the realm of collaboration. Staff can lend useful insight into a person's leadership and management style. Peers can speak to communication style and what it's like to work with the person. Customers can be useful, too, especially in public-facing roles like sales or customer service. Customers can tell you if your candidate added value to their business. Vendors can be useful; they will give you some insight into how the candidate treats others. If I'm hiring someone in accounts payable, finance, or accounting, I'll speak with vendors they've worked with in the past. I want to see that they partner with vendors to solve problems and advance the business.

BACKDOOR REFERENCES ARE EVEN BETTER

Backdoor references are gold. These are people you find on your own—names the candidate didn't provide. They're the most revealing and useful, and a wise investment of your time.

Some wonder if this is ethical or legal. Absolutely. It's standard procedure, in fact. We're not talking about asking questions that are illegal or untoward. Veteran headhunters do this all the time; it's part of our standard process. It should be part of yours, as well. That said, use extreme discretion to not breach confidentiality if the candidate's job search is not public.

By now, LinkedIn should be your best friend. Learn how to use LinkedIn's Advanced Search function. It gives you the ability to track down former managers, co-workers, customers, competitors, the media, etc. All kinds of people will surface.

Tell them: "You weren't given as a reference, but I noticed on LinkedIn that you're connected to John. I'd really appreciate a few minutes of your time, before I make this important hiring decision." Explain who you are and emphasize discretion.

If more than a few handful of people are hesitant to chat with you, that's indicative of something.

KEY QUESTIONS

Once you have a reference on the phone, thank them for connecting with you. Tell them you need just fifteen minutes and that everything will be held in confidence—you're not going to share their feedback with the candidate (and honor this, of course). Tell them you're looking for themes and patterns. You can say, "I've almost made my decision. This phone call is a good way for me to confirm my decision and learn the best ways to get the most out of him." That disarms the interaction and allows for a more candid reference.

Here are the questions I recommend, in the following order:

1. "Give me some context. Tell me a bit about how you worked together. When was that?" You're seeking confirmation of the dates and reporting structure.
2. "Tell me a bit about the role they were in." Again, we're validating the scope of the role that the candidate described.
3. "As you know, I'm talking to (candidate's name) about a (type of) role. It will require these competencies (list the three to five key competencies from the Scorecard). To begin with, how would you say she rates on those competencies?"
4. "What metrics did you use to measure her performance? Was she measured on revenue growth, cost reduction, number of new customers signed, etc.?" This will provide insight into what she was asked to do in that role and how that compares to what you're going to be asking of her.
5. "How did she achieve these results? How was her performance?" Don't accept generalities; keep digging. You are looking for specific examples.
6. "At the time you worked together, what were her strengths and weaknesses?" Define strengths as areas where she was in the top 10 percent. "In what areas would you say she's in the bottom 10 percent?"
7. "How did she compare with the rest of your staff? Was she in the top 5 percent? Top 50 percent?"

8. "Tell me about what led to her departure." We're looking for why and when she left the company. And importantly, whether the facts presented align with what the candidate shared earlier.
9. "What's the one thing she could have done to be more effective?" Don't fill the awkward silence. If they say they can't think of anything, say, "It's okay, I don't mind waiting a moment while you think about it."
10. If you're filling a manager role, ask: "How would you describe her as a leader of people? What's her style? How did her staff respond to her?"
11. "Would you enthusiastically re-hire her again today?" I'm looking for "definitely" or "absolutely" without hesitation.
12. "On a scale of 1 to 10, compared to all the people you've ever hired, how would you rate her?" You want to hear "8, 9, or 10." Anything less than an 8 is a red flag, because they're likely being generous.

Reference checking must be done in a phone call. People will not put negative things in writing, so don't try to cut corners with a reference check via email. Keep the call to fifteen to twenty minutes and offer to return the favor any way you can.

THE NECESSITY OF BACKGROUND CHECKS

A background check is different from a reference check. They're used to validate the candidate's education, criminal history, credit history, drug use, etc. Fortunately, this previously costly process is now a modest investment for all new hires. I recommend HireRight based in Irvine, California; they're relatively inexpensive and fast.

In my experience, 2 percent of background checks at this stage will identify a deal-breaker issue. It's heartbreaking. Early this year, I nearly placed a phenomenal candidate in a VP of marketing role. She had great interviews, a kickass Test Drive, outstanding reference checks, and an MBA from a top school. The background check, however, revealed that she never graduated from her undergraduate program; she was just a few credits shy. Here's the kicker: Had she told us this in advance, we would have paid it no mind. Education is not highly predictive of success, remember? But once we learned of this omission, her entire story was then thrown into question. What else wasn't she telling us? We've all seen CEOs let go after it's been revealed that they lied on their résumé about a degree. The most common issue is that someone studied at a school but never completed the degree. Sometimes, you'll miss this subtlety on their résumé; other times, the résumé incorrectly states that their studies were completed.

In this chapter, we talked about the importance of checking references, how a candidate's resistance to provide references is a red flag, and how backdoor references are a great source of unbiased information.

In the next chapter, we'll talk about making an irresistible offer that gets the "Yes."

CHAPTER 8

THE OFFER THEY CAN'T REFUSE

||||||||||||||||||||

In the summer of 2015, I conducted a search for a New York-based chief marketing officer. After two months, I found a remarkably talented woman. My client and I followed the process you've read thus far: background checks, reference checks, the interviews, and the Test Drive, the whole enchilada. She truly was a Rockstar.

And then my nightmare began. Over a weekend in late August, my client impulsively emailed the candidate an offer, without having me review it first. You would think this wouldn't be a big issue, but it nearly killed the whole deal.

In the letter, my client changed the proposed title from chief marketing officer to VP of marketing because he didn't want to demotivate his VP of sales during a crucial selling month.

He changed the start date that he had discussed with the candidate, moving it up a week because he was overeager to get her onboard. He neglected to include information about benefits, which were important to her because she was the primary breadwinner of her family. And the letter was vague about how the variable compensation program worked.

As you'd expect, I spent a weekend getting the finalist back in the boat—undoing the damage from an ill-advised offer letter. It was an amateurish mistake but all too common. We saved the deal, she accepted the offer, and she's doing great.

The point is that you've done too much work during the recruiting process to make a mistake at the job offer stage, and to not do everything possible to reel the finalist into your boat.

According to a recent study by Jobvite, 89 percent is the average offer acceptance rate in the United States. For Rockstars, it's considerably lower because they are highly selective and in demand—I'd estimate closer to two-thirds. Once they're engaged in a discussion with you, they tend to shop around a bit, just like someone in the market to purchase a new home. During this window, they are "in play." They will come up with their first, second, and third choices. That's an extra challenge in dealing with Rockstars—it's not solely your decision to make. Unlike with B-Players, everything during the offer process must go flawlessly.

When you call someone's references, you've inadvertently put them in play. Several times a year, I call references and then my candidate's former manager contacts them, saying, "I didn't know you were open to an opportunity. I want to speak to you about this job that just opened up." Sure enough, my candidate takes that position instead, because they liked working with that manager. It's arrogant to assume that candidates should consider themselves lucky to receive an offer from you. You can do that with B- and C-Players but not Rockstars. It's time to treat them as a rare breed—because they are.

In these pages, we've talked extensively about de-risking your hire. When preparing an offer, think about how to remove the risk for the candidate. Consider the questions they might have: Will I enjoy it? Will I fit? Will the manager and I get along? Will the job really be as described? Am I clear on what I'll be paid? Think about the times you've made a career move, with all the uncertainty it entails. It pays to know what other jobs the candidate might be considering. It's okay to ask them about this in the career exploration portion of the interview. Think about how your position compares to any others they are considering and present yours in the best possible light. Don't oversell or deceive; be accurate but make it as compelling as possible. And if you lack selling skills, find someone in your organization who can invest time with the finalist to reel them into the boat.

Be patient. Don't get upset when the candidate asks a question or raises an issue about the offer. Often, my clients expect to get an immediate "Yes" after sending the offer. That won't happen with Rockstars. Know your non-negotiables, bite your tongue, and be patient. Don't get emotional or frustrated with the candidate. This is a business negotiation, it's not personal. It's the time where a third-party go-between adds a lot of value, by keeping the emotion out of it.

It's a shame, but countless hiring managers mess this up at the five-yard line. It doesn't have to be that way. Follow the guidelines in this chapter and you'll avoid the mistakes and land your first-choice candidate.

THE TRIAL CLOSE

After the Test Drive, but before investing massive time in reference checks, it's time to do a trial close. This is something that every good sales rep does with their prospective customer. The purpose is to test the prospect's genuine level of interest and understand their remaining concerns. You want to know how interested and engaged your candidate is, as well as if you're on the same page financially. You should do this in person if at all possible. It's harder for a candidate to decline an offer given in person than in a cold email. Be warm and enthusiastic; tell them how great working together will be; share your vision of what your relationship could look like.

It's a short conversation in which you say how much you

enjoyed meeting with them in the interviews and how well they did in the Test Drive. During the trial close, make sure you're on the same page about scope, timing, title, compensation, and other essential elements. Take the time in advance to make notes for yourself, so that you touch on everything. When presenting the potential offer in the trial close, say: "Presuming everything checks out in the references, which I assume it will, I'd love to have you join our organization as our next VP of marketing. We intend to put together an offer letter by Tuesday. Based on what I've seen, I think you'll do incredibly well. I know you'll enjoy it and do the best work of your career. Plus, I think you'll be a great fit for the organization. I'm convinced you have the competencies to be successful in the role. I'm going to let you handpick your own team. The compensation is exactly as we've discussed, which is (XYZ, and here are some of the key terms). Presuming I put that together, are you prepared to accept?"

Then, be silent. Note the candidate's response. Are they enthusiastic? Do they have objections you can address, negotiation points you can resolve, clarifications you need to make? Facial cues are important. Reassure them that you genuinely see a great match; you think it's going to be a great relationship, and that the risk is very low of it not working out. Reduce their perceived risk.

In addition to compensation, talk about growth and challenge. Remember, Rockstars crave challenge even more than money. Explain that you're committed to making this the most engaging, interesting role they've ever held and the greatest career challenge they've ever faced. Say: "I know you're up to it. That's why we've chosen you. That's why I want you on my team." Show the love.

To provide context, I even explain the search process to the finalist. I explain that, "We've been looking for four months. We've looked at 175 people. You're the one." This conveys that you are incredibly selective, which not only appeals to their ego but also confirms that they'll be working with other Rockstars. Go back to the Job Invitation, too, to remind yourself what you touted as great about this opportunity— you'll learn from one of our best managers, you won't have a ton of travel, we'll give you this training, etc. Restate the selling points.

This is also the time to review your notes from the first phone screen with the candidate. Look back to see how they answered, "What is annoying or frustrating or missing in your current role?" This is when you remind your candidate of the pain they're feeling and how much it's costing them, just like a sales rep does with a potential customer. Refresh them on their endless commute, poor treatment by their micromanager, and lack of equity participation.

Use this time to restate and articulate the responsibilities of the job, setting expectations. Say something like: "Here's what I'm asking you to do: Come in to launch this division/build our brand/turn around this sales team, and here are the key priorities I envision in the first three months and twelve months." This serves to ensure you're on the same page and to present what a great challenge you have in store for them. Rockstars respond to this. Be sure to use the words: "I want you on my team." We all want to be wanted, no matter the size of our ego.

I highly recommend that you—the hiring manager—present the offer yourself; don't have HR or your outside headhunter do it. The hiring manager speaks with a unique type of affection and enthusiasm for the candidate—it's the beginning of a relationship, following a weeks-long courtship. If the candidate is being pursued by two or three companies, the personal offer from the hiring manager can make all the difference. You may be tempted to have a third party do it—to avoid the uncomfortable questions or negotiation—or to provide you with time to develop answers to their counteroffer. Don't do it.

Next, lay out the compensation. Don't put it in writing yet; get the verbal "Yes" before putting pen to paper. Say: "I'd like to take you through the compensation package, or remuneration structure." Don't use the word "offer" because that implies you expect a counteroffer and are opening the door to a negotiation. Go through the compensation structure slowly and methodically; don't leave anything out. There's the fixed salary, variable compensation (does it have a cap? how does it work?), equity (what percentage? how does it vest? how much could that be worth over time in different scenarios?), benefits, health care, vacation allowance, travel allowance, training, and any other perks such as executive coaching. Write them down ahead of time for your own reference so you don't leave anything out. The list is likely far more impressive than you recall, when you include every element of value.

Next is the trial close. Say: "Presuming we put together a program that has all that I've talked about and we agree on the role and responsibilities, what is your interest level?" That tells the candidate it's time to give feedback. If it's anything other than an emphatic "I'm in!" find out why. They may say, "I need to discuss it with my spouse." Okay. I offer to have dinner with them and their spouse, I can get them over the hump if I meet face to face. If they say, "I need to sleep on it," ask about their concerns. If they say, "We're totally on a different page financially," express your surprise because compensation was discussed from the very first call. You shouldn't be on a different page at this point. This may signal that they've been playing games or shopping around for an offer. If that's the case, you've saved yourself the time you would have spent on reference checks and putting the offer in writing.

As with any sale, you're more likely to have success if there is a deadline. Don't threaten or bully the candidate to decide, but do let them know there is a backup candidate. You *always* have a backup candidate. And this is why. Say: "You're the one I want. At the same time, I have a business to run. I have a backup candidate who's viable and very interested. We need to agree now on when you'll be able to make a decision and what additional information I can provide to help you make that decision."

If they say, "I just need to talk to my spouse," you can say, "Great. Why don't we get together? I'll bring along my wife. The four of us can get together and talk about it."

If they say, "I want to review the financials again," say, "Great. Let's set up a time with the CFO. She'll sit down and take you through how much cash we have and how long it lasts."

If they say, "I've got another offer that I'm expecting by Thursday," say, "Great. I totally understand that someone like you is in demand. Let's set up a time on Friday to talk about how they compare and if there are any adjustments I need to make to our offer to make it an easy decision for you."

If the candidate wants to ride along with a sales rep, make it happen. Quickly. If they want to meet some Board members, say, "Yes." You can say, "I will make anything available to you, but we need to agree that by Thursday we'll make a decision to either sign or part ways." Unless you create the sense of importance of a deadline, these final steps can drag out unnecessarily.

If a candidate wants to negotiate salary, remember the impact this person can make in your organization and remember the cost of the vacancy. If you lose this person over $5,000 and that seat remains open for another six months until you find another Rockstar, you just made a poor financial decision.

Be creative, though, when negotiating compensation. If a candidate asks for a salary of $100,000 and for whatever reason you can't exceed $90,000, it's okay to say, "I can't do that and here's why, but I can do this." Then, offer more in variable cash, bonuses, commission, a one-time signing bonus, equity, time off, etc. They might say, "Wow, an extra week off? I didn't get that $10,000, but I did get an extra week of vacation." In my experience, when there's a reasonably small gap (10 percent or less), there are creative ways to close it in almost all cases.

If a candidate asks for several things they'd like changed, listen to the entire list first (do not comment on each one yet), then ask with another trial close, "If I can do all these things, are you prepared to accept today?" If there's something on their list you can't do, you can say, "That list is very reasonable. Unfortunately, I can't do number four. Here's what I can do. If I do, are you prepared to accept today?" Always be closing.

Don't get frustrated, unless the candidate behaves in a way that's inconsistent with your company's DNA. If they are rude or threatening or arrogant, you can factor this into your decision and move to your backup candidate. These can be tense discussions, but if the candidate handles them in a constructive, thoughtful, methodical way, you'll come to admire their confidence. Rockstars are worth the investment.

PUT IT IN WRITING

Only once they have verbally accepted do I recommend drafting the written offer letter. The written letter is a formality that reflects everything the candidate has already agreed to. Put an expiration date on the letter—twenty-four to thirty-six hours from the time they receive it. They've already said, "Yes," so this expiration date shouldn't be a problem.

Above all, be sure there are no surprises in the letter. If you are having someone from human resources write the letter, be sure you've read it before it goes to the candidate. I see many offer letters that are cold, terse, and uninspiring—likely written by an attorney, and the businesspeople didn't push back. Have your attorney review your offer letter, of course, but make the letter warm. You're inviting this person to your home, to your family. The letter should enthusiastically welcome and congratulate them. They've won the long, arduous beauty contest.

THE DEADLY RISK OF A COUNTEROFFER

When it comes to Rockstars, the risk of a counteroffer from your candidate's current employer is something that must be on your radar. It doesn't happen often (10–20 percent of the time), but enough that it's worth anticipating and addressing in advance. The reason they get a counteroffer, of course, is because their current employer knows they're a Rockstar. B- and C-Players rarely get counteroffers, so this is another hurdle you face when you deal with Rockstars.

Once the candidate signs and returns your offer letter, and before they give notice to their current employer, address the risk of a counteroffer head-on. To do that, have an explicit discussion. Once they've received the counteroffer, it may be too late. When discussing a start date with the finalist, say, "Great. June 13 works for us. We'll have your office set up and be ready for you. Let's talk about the timing between now and then. On what date do you plan to resign?" Many times, candidates will say they haven't thought about it. So, you can say, "Great. Let's talk it through." Or maybe they have a plan for when and how. Just be sure you have a formal discussion about it. Leave nothing to chance—you want to be with the candidate when they think through the plan of their departure.

Next, ask them if they anticipate receiving a counteroffer from their current employer. If they say no, let them know it may happen—prepare them. Remind them how disappointing it can be to take giving notice for their employer to finally step up and provide what they felt they deserved all along. Ask them: "How will you handle that situation?" You hope they'll say they won't even consider it, but they might say, "That's a good question." If that happens, you advise them, "Well, I'm glad we're talking about it. Before I go through the hassle of putting together an offer letter and letting the other candidate go, I need to understand that you're in the boat. If you're not sure, let's hold off on the offer letter and figure out how to get confident that you're in the boat."

Educate the candidate that 90 percent of the time, when someone accepts a counteroffer, they are gone from the company within a year. It's because emotionally they already had one foot out the door and because they resent having to essentially threaten to leave. What's more, the company often feels they can no longer count on the person for any length of time. Because your candidate may not have experienced this, explain why accepting a counteroffer is always a mistake. It starts the clock ticking on the end of their time with their company—and of course, the great opportunity you're presenting them will be gone.

If it seems like they need it, offer to help them any way you can. Offer to have them call you right before they meet with their boss to resign. Some moral support helps. Touch base with them on the day they were to resign and ask how it went. Again, hopefully, their answer is reassuring. If they say they're expecting a counteroffer but won't even look at it, great. If they say they owe it to their company to at least look at the counteroffer, that's a red flag. Be ready and don't let a day go by without speaking live with your finalist until you know their resignation has been accepted and their final date set.

DON'T FORGET THE OTHER HALF

Hiring managers also tend to forget the candidate's spouse or partner. They, too, need to be onboard, or it can tank the deal. If a spouse is risk-averse to change or has concerns about the stability of the company, the deal can go south. A spouse may also have a social circle tied to the current company, or if a relocation is involved, be concerned about their children changing schools particularly mid-year. Before the Test Drive, ask the candidate how their spouse feels about this job opportunity. When it's time for the trial close, offer to meet him or her; invite them into the office, have your own spouse or partner join you and then go out to dinner. When you make it personal, it goes beyond an offer letter. Sometimes by winning the spouse, I win over the Rockstar.

PULL OUT ALL THE STOPS

Even if you've gotten the signed offer letter, the candidate is still at risk until the day they show up for work. Have your

CEO call to congratulate and welcome them to the family. Invite them to spend some time at your office; maybe invite them to key meetings so they can begin to understand some of the issues you're working on. You may want to start copying them on emails (once they've signed a non-disclosure agreement, of course). Make it a team effort. Have them meet their team, their peers, the investors, the Board. Pull them in the boat; it will be harder for them to change their mind. Send them a welcome gift. Make it something personal, so they know you thought about it. I also recommend giving them a copy of **The First 90 Days** by Michael Watkins, which outlines how a new hire can get off to a fast start in the new role.

START DATES

How far out should a start date be? That's part of the negotiation, and some people will need longer than others. It's customary to give an employer at least two weeks' notice, but some people will have extended projects they need to wrap up, and that requires more time. A start date can be as far out as three months.

In this chapter, we talked about the necessity of discussing the offer in person, setting clear expectations about the position, and using the information you've gathered throughout the process to compare their current position to your opening.

In the next chapter, we'll talk about what to do once they've accepted the offer and arrived for their first day of work: onboarding the new employee.

PART III

GROW YOUR ROCKSTARS

CHAPTER 9

GET THE FIRST THIRTY DAYS RIGHT

||||||||||||||||||||||

This winter, I worked with a client who hired a new VP of sales and threw him into things far too quickly. In the first week, my client put him in front of a potential customer before the new guy was familiar with the products or understood the subtleties of the role. He didn't know the competition and wasn't from the industry. Most importantly, he didn't understand the context surrounding this prospective customer; he didn't know what had already transpired. He did his best, but it was clear that he wasn't prepared to face the market.

My client regretted the decision to move prematurely, and apologized to both the new hire and to the prospective client.

He said he was so excited about the new employee that he couldn't wait to involve him in the discussion. Fortunately, the client appreciated his candor and the deal was saved.

But it might not have been.

Don't risk it. It's common for an executive to throw a new Rockstar into the deep end, believing that she can swim. Be careful about throwing a new employee into the water too soon, though. There are risks.

MISCONCEPTIONS OF HIRING MANAGERS

Do any of these sound familiar?

- ★ "We don't have time to onboard. We've got to get them producing."
- ★ "They'll figure it out as they go. We're really small. How hard could it be?"
- ★ "We only hire Rockstars who are super smart, so they'll figure it out."
- ★ "They filled out all the paperwork, so they're onboarded."

The moral of this chapter is as goes the first thirty days, so goes the employer/employee relationship.

THE CRUCIAL FIRST MONTHS

The first three to six months are when new hires are particularly susceptible to turnover, according to a Society for Human Resource Management study. Companies lose 17 percent of their new hires within the first three months. In fact, 4 percent of new employees don't return for a second day of work!

This can be prevented, however. According to a 2014 study by Bamboo HR, 23 percent of people who left within the first three months said they wouldn't have left if they'd just received clear guidance on their job responsibilities. Twenty-one percent said they wanted more effective training and 17 percent said friendlier co-worker interaction would have made the difference.

The key is to remember a few things: one, even Rockstars need to be oriented, and two, during the crucial first few months, you're still selling. The new employee doesn't have much invested during the first month, so they're watching to see two things: first, if you have your act together as an organization and second, how committed you are to their long-term success.

They want to see if you are invested in them and if you follow through on the commitments made during the interview process. The employer/employee bond was damaged irreparably a couple of decades ago. And now that employees no longer count on lifetime employment, they no longer offer lifetime loyalty. As soon as you start showing that you don't have your act together or that you're not committed to their long-term success, they will not hesitate to jump ship. This begins by properly onboarding each new Rockstar.

THE IMPORTANCE OF ONBOARDING

While it's true that Rockstars ramp up more rapidly, they still need to be oriented to the business. It's shortsighted to bypass training they need at this point because you've invested so much time in the recruiting process. Remember that if this new hire leaves after a week or a month, you've already released your backup candidate. You'll have to start the whole process over by finding 150 new viable candidates to refill your pipeline. I've been there. In a word, it sucks.

Successful onboarding isn't rocket science. It's a period when your new employee needs to be taught the things they'll need to know to be successful. It's not just, "Here's the bathroom. Here's your website login. Get started." You need to teach them not only how to perform but also about the company's values. Bad habits can form quickly if your expectations about behavior and performance are not articulated.

Go slow to go fast. Every hour you invest in onboarding pays off down the road. Of course, if you can onboard several people at once, it's a great leverage of time. I work with my clients to have all new employees start on the first Monday of each month, or every other Monday.

So, what needs to be covered during onboarding? Whether formally or informally, there are vital areas. The more forethought, documentation, and rehearsal you can put into these, the better they scale and can be re-used with new hires (updated on occasion).

THE ROLE ITSELF

Be sure that your new Rockstar is clear on the role they've accepted. Go over the role (yes, again), the responsibilities, and the priorities. Point by point. Invest the time to ensure they are crystal clear. Flesh out all the things you discussed during the recruiting process. If one of the responsibilities is to build a process that ensures fewer bugs in the software, talk about what that means and what the goal is. Provide a target and timeframe.

CONSTRAINTS

Also, talk about constraints. Does the employee have a budget? Can they make hires—whether employees or consultants? Who will approve those hires, and how?

PRIORITIES

If you fail to prioritize for your new Rockstar, they'll use their best judgment. But that isn't yet informed by the realities of your business situation. Tell them the things you want them to focus on during the first week, first month, and first quarter. Equally importantly, tell them why. Get their buy-in to the plan of attack.

COMMUNICATION

How are you going to communicate? Each company—and each manager—has a rhythm. The new hire needs to know how to communicate up, down, and sideways. They also need to be aware of expectations about attending standing meetings, providing weekly reports, give you a heads-up on bad news, and the like. Whatever your communication preferences are, set them now. The onus is on you, and the best hiring managers start good habits from day one.

It's also important to ask the new hire how they prefer to communicate. Some people are better in person, others on the phone, or in writing. Some prefer groups, others individual conversations. If you know their preferences, you can adjust accordingly.

THE BUSINESS

Make sure they understand the company's mission, vision,

history, priorities, and the main initiatives the business is focused on. Educate every single employee—regardless of role or level—on the financials. How much money the business makes, your margins, variable costs, fixed costs, how you make a profit, cash in the bank, etc. There's no reason anyone in the company, from CEO to receptionist, shouldn't understand the basic financials of the business.

Company meetings are a great time to make sure everyone has this information. Done properly, it shouldn't take more than an hour. You'd be shocked by how few employers help their people know the numbers.

THE TEAM

Who does what? What are the key functions? Who are the leaders of those functions? What's important to them? What are the key responsibilities?

CULTURE

What's expected of the new hire, in terms of values and DNA? What is not tolerated? How do we function as a company? What does bad behavior look like? Provide recent examples—no names necessary—of Rockstars who were shown the door for violating the culture, regardless of their outstanding performance.

COMPETITION

Who is our competition? How many others are there? What's the market share? On what basis do they compete? Who tries to be the low-cost provider? Who tries to be a high-service company? How do we differentiate ourselves?

SALES AND MARKETING

What are our key messages? Who are our target customers? How do we acquire customer leads and convert those leads? Advertising? Email? Referrals? How do we keep customers? What are the customers' concerns, objections, and fears? Everyone in the company is a salesperson. They can't sell if they don't understand the key messages.

THE PRODUCT

Teach your new Rockstar about the products you sell. Pricing, features, benefits, functionality. I was fortunate years ago to serve as the first Vice President of Marketing for Dyson, the large consumer products maker. One of our culture rites of passage was that, during their first week, every new employee was required to take apart a Dyson vacuum and reassemble it—to understand how it works from the inside out. If your product is software, provide hands-on demos. If it's an intangible service, teach them how the experience works. Reinforce this knowledge constantly, particularly around new-product launches.

CAREER ASPIRATIONS

In addition to training on matters relating to the business, the onboarding period is also the time to understand your new hires' aspirations. I tell my employees they've hopped on our company train and that my job as their manager is to keep them on our train for as long as possible. That said, I'll acknowledge that it's probably not going to be the last train they ride and that's okay.

Tell them that whether they stay two years, five years, or ten years, you want to maximize that time and make sure they learn and grow and see it as beneficial to their career. To do that, you need to understand their career aspirations. Find out where they want to grow. Do they want to improve at leading people? Do they want to work internationally? Start their own company one day? You can't own their career, but you can help them by providing opportunities consistent with what they want to do long term.

DELIVERY

There are countless ways to deliver the onboarding training. You get to pick and choose the most effective method based on the topic and how many people you're training at the same time.

How you teach your new employee these things will vary. Common topics such as product knowledge can be done in an interactive group setting, while expectations of a particular role will be an individual conversation. Ask questions. Allow new hires to come to their own conclusions. Use quizzes to reinforce the material.

Individual training will cover career aspirations, roles, and responsibilities. Videos are effective if they're interesting. For larger companies, share a video of the CEO speaking about the company's key initiatives and mission. Before the start date, give the new hire some pre-reading; it can be case studies of customers, timelines of new projects, or industry reports. Anything you might give to a prospective or current customer (sales brochure, product data, sales contract, instructions on how to use a product) should be provided to a new hire so they can read and understand them, too.

CADENCE

Be clear with your new hire as to when you expect them to be up to speed. Let them know it doesn't need to be within the first day or week or month. But within three months, they should be at least 80 percent ramped. During the first month, they're crawling while they observe, attend meetings, and start to make contributions as they put the pieces together. Within the first quarter, they're walking, starting to deliver on some individual assignments. After a quarter, they should be up and running.

WEEKLY 1:1 CHECK-INS

The weekly 1:1 is a vital part of the employee experience, and even Rockstars need them. Particularly as the person is getting ramped up, here are some questions to ask:

★ "How are you feeling in your new job? Are you feeling confident or shaky? Are you nervous?"

★ "What are you enjoying the most?"

★ "What's the piece you're most excited about?"

★ "Is it what you expected?" This is important. If they say no, you've got a potential early departure. Say: "Let's work together to figure out how to make it more of what you expected" or "Let's agree that we made a mistake and see if there's another role in the company that could be up your alley."

★ "Has anything surprised you?"

★ "Do you have everything you need?"

★ "Is there anything that's unclear?"

★ "What else can I do to make you more successful? Do you need more of my time? Do you need less guidance?"

You don't want someone to depart whom you didn't even know was unhappy. Getting feedback early and often is key. You are also assessing them. How's their performance? The work itself? Their pace, quality, decision making, judgment? How are their values? Is their DNA what you thought it was?

Still unsure if onboarding is time well spent? According to

a recent study by the Aberdeen Group, 66 percent of companies with an onboarding program report a higher rate of successful assimilation of new hires into the company culture and a faster time to productivity. Go slow to go fast.

EARLY WARNING SIGNS

From day one, I'm looking for three things: skill, will, and DNA. Within a month, you should be able to confirm whether the competencies you identified in the interview process are there, whether they truly want to do the work, and if the DNA you identified is as it seemed. If you've done a good job interviewing and hiring, you should have an 80 or 90 percent success rate. And congratulate yourself, because you're nearly twice as effective as the national average.

But if you see early warning signs, it's time to redouble your efforts to save the relationship. You've invested so much time and expense. Determine if the person is a Rockstar but just has issues that can be addressed. If it's a skill issue, are the competencies there? Can he do the job? Often, you can train the person and enhance his skills, or reassign him to a different position.

If will is the problem, you'll have to figure out what the issue is; why don't they want to do the work? You can see if something is de-motivating them, or if they're just in the wrong seat on the bus.

DNA is the toughest disconnect to resolve. When you have a DNA mismatch, it's nearly impossible to turn things around. Don't wait to have the discussion with them. Outline examples of behaviors that aren't aligning with the company's. Convey that you're concerned you made a hiring mistake, and discuss whether the situation can change. Fast.

WHAT TO DO WHEN YOU'VE MADE A BAD HIRE

Commit to exiting your underperformers and your mis-hires. Be clear on the difference between the two—an underperformer may or may not have the DNA; they may or may not be a culture fit. A mis-hire is someone who doesn't share the DNA of the company, so even if they are performing, they need to go.

Most executives will look the other way when someone is performing, yet doesn't share the DNA. That's a huge problem because the person's bad behavior becomes cancerous to the rest of the company. It spreads.

In most cases, you should be able to decide within the first thirty days whether you've made a hiring mistake. It's not in anyone's best interest to defer the decision to let someone go. The solution is to use a diagnostic assessment and then make the decision. If the decision is to part ways, own it. If the decision is to try to make it work, own that, too.

The diagnostic has several questions:

- ★ Do they have the will? Do they have the desire to do the job?
- ★ Do they have the skill?
- ★ Have you provided direct feedback?
- ★ Do you see the trajectory changing?
- ★ Are other employees telling you the person is in over their head?
- ★ Are you spending a disproportionate amount of your time on that person?
- ★ Is there a different role in the company where they might excel?

HOW TO LET SOMEONE GO

You've made a hiring mistake. Own it. Don't blame the candidate.

You're actually doing the person a favor. If you've genuinely made a hiring mistake, what good is it to keep the person around, under the illusion that they're doing well? It's actually cruel and selfish to avoid the conversation. It's far better to have the discussion early on when the employee might still have other job opportunities they could reactivate. Offer to make introductions on their behalf. You may not be able to provide a positive reference because they haven't been there long enough, but imagine if you do keep them on for a year or two. Now, that would be cruel.

The key is to convince yourself that you're doing both parties a favor. You need to believe that you're freeing them up to find a home that's a better fit. Upon their exit, do not throw the person under the bus; do not badmouth them to your other employees. Everyone's going to be watching you. Be courteous, humane, and gracious.

I've found that more often than not, the employee actually feels relieved. They probably knew they were flailing and will agree with you that it was a mis-hire. If they didn't know they were flailing, then you have failed as a manager. No one should ever be surprised when they are let go. That means you must have multiple conversations before the one where you actually release them. They might not agree with you or like what they're hearing, but you need to point out to them how their behavior is different than your expectations. Be gracious but be clear that this isn't going to work.

Before you have the final discussion, speak with your HR partner or your company's employment attorney. You need to let someone go by the book, particularly if they're in a protected class. Document the discussions you've had along the way. I usually email that to the employee, saying something like, "I wanted to summarize what we discussed today when we got together." And then recap the conversation, noting the behavior that needs to change and offering to help the person do that. These emails will form a defensible paper trail that a lawyer might later ask to see.

Here's how to part ways with a mis-hire:

* When you've done everything previously mentioned and the time has come, be kind, respectful, and humane.
* Be brief and know what you're going to say. This should be a five-minute meeting. Once you tell them of your decision, they're not listening to much else.
* It's always in person, unless absolutely unavoidable. Even if that means you flying across the country to part ways with a sales rep, do it. You owe that to them, and they are far less likely to feel mistreated if you have this conversation in person.
* Be firm; this isn't a debate or a discussion. Say you've made the decision to part ways because of the reasons you've discussed.
* You're the hiring manager; you should be the firing manager. Do not delegate this to HR.
* Be sure to do it in a private place to preserve their dignity and minimize the disruption. It should not be in a glass fishbowl conference room, in full view of others.
* After it's done, notify the rest of your team. Don't provide details. Say something like, "So-and-so is going to be leaving us. His last day is Friday. We wish him nothing but the best in his endeavors. If you have any questions about work and coverage, let me know. In the meantime, we've already begun a recruiting process to fill the position promptly." Most of the time, your team will already know why that person is leaving. Many will ask what took you so long. That

should be a good reminder that your gut is usually right when it comes to firing (but not when it comes to hiring). When you smell smoke, there is usually a fire.

In this chapter, we've talked about how even Rockstars need onboarding, how to give them everything they need to be successful and how to exit mis-hires and underperformers quickly.

In the next and final chapter, we'll talk about how to ensure that Rockstars keep rocking at your company.

CHAPTER 10

GIVE ROCKSTARS WHAT THEY CRAVE

|||||||||||||||||||||||

It takes forethought, planning, and consistency to lead Rockstars. You can expect a lot out of them. But they have high expectations of you, too. It doesn't mean you need to be smarter in all domains, but it means you must serve them and provide leadership.

A book about recruiting Rockstars can't end before sharing the things this rare breed will and won't respond to. Those things drive retention—which means ironically that you'll need to recruit fewer people over time.

CREATING A GREAT PLACE TO WORK

Because Rockstars have the luxury of choosing a home

where they feel they can do their best work, it's vital that you provide such a place. If your company is like most, you have a ways to go on this dimension. As with recruiting Rockstars, you choose to *do* this or *not* do this. But you can't do it half-ass. As a four-time entrepreneur, I've found that every hour and effort I've invested in building a great place to work makes my recruiting job that much easier. It doesn't require paying top dollar. It doesn't require the sexiest office space. It simply demands a commitment by you and your leadership team to doing the things to attract and enable your Rockstars to do great work, and then get out of their way.

I have the good fortune of serving as Chairman of Retrofit, the Chicago-based online healthcare company I started five years ago. We have sixty remarkable employees and have won numerous awards for being among the nation's best places to work (including an award for best workplaces for women). Here are a few examples of the programs that have made it possible:

FREE PRODUCT

Retrofit provides an opportunity for each team member to participate in the company's weight-management program. Each receives a live coach, a smart app, a wireless tracker, and digital body scale. They also get access to expert-led online classes, and social support from an online community where employees can engage with each other and post updates to keep each other healthy.

UNLIMITED VACATION POLICY

As a healthy lifestyle company, Retrofit understands that happier employees are more productive. We want our folks to be able to enjoy the things they love to do. So, our unlimited vacation policy allows employees to take off as much time as they need, as long as they complete their work or arrange for coverage while they're out. We also provide the day off for birthdays and a *Retrofit Recharge* week where employees take time off to refill their battery.

WORK FROM ANYWHERE

Although based in Chicago, Retrofit has employees across the country. And they can work from wherever they feel most productive. This means less windshield time and more time for the things that make us happy. We even celebrate the holidays with a virtual online party.

FLEXIBLE HOURS

We make it as easy as possible for our employees to seamlessly integrate their work and their life. We have both full-time and part-time employees; some work early or late. This allows us to best serve our clients and customers, while providing flexibility to our employees. It makes a huge impact to think about the entire person, not just the employee part of the person.

HEALTHY WORKPLACE

We know that part of a healthy lifestyle is moving throughout the day. We encourage our employees to get up and get moving. Our office space includes treadmill desks and standing desks. We offer regular employee walking challenges to encourage employees to get moving, and we take breaks for yoga during company meetings.

HEALTHY FOOD

Of course, complimentary fruit and other healthy treats are on hand to give employees the energy they need to perform and feel great—not the constant supply of sugar provided by some employers.

GOOD EGG DAYS

"Be a good egg" has been part of Retrofit's core DNA from day one, so we look for people who truly *are* good eggs. Employees are encouraged to take off one day each quarter to make a difference in their communities through volunteerism.

WORTH EVERY PENNY

Now we begin to come full circle with the beginning of this book. There, I implored you to devote 30 to 50 percent of your time to the people part of your business. When you hire Rockstars, you spend less time motivating and managing. Even though you'll spend 30 to 50 percent of your time hiring, leading, and inspiring, it saves you time in the long run because you'll no longer have to micromanage, motivate, and babysit B- and C-Players. You can spend your time looking forward, rather than feeling stuck managing today. It allows you to build an organization that's driving forward into the future. Rockstars make that possible.

There are downsides to hiring Rockstars, however. These factors shouldn't dissuade you, but they are worth understanding.

★ *Hard to find.* Finding Rockstars is far more difficult than finding B- or C-Players. You must be willing to avoid settling when you're hiring for a position. Because the recruiting might take longer, it means the rest of your employees need to fill in and pinch hit, likely doing extra work to compensate for the vacancy. Rockstars are willing to do that extra work if it means you don't hire a B- or C-Player to join their team. They will become frustrated, though, if you have a significant number of vacancies for a long time—so do your part, which is recruiting.

★ *High expectations.* Rockstars also have high expectations of your leadership. They will hold you accountable. If you're not doing a good job as their leader, they will call you on it (B- and C-Players won't). This will absolutely make you a better leader over time, but you need the stomach for feedback and critique.

★ *Rockstar-conducive environment.* If you're not good with servant leadership and following your people—if you must be the smartest one in the room—Rockstars won't mesh well with you. They don't work under command-and-control structures, so they won't stay.

★ *Career challenge.* Rockstars expect career advancement. They will leave you when you don't provide them with stretch and a career path, or when you fail to recognize their contributions. Your goal as the manager is to keep the Rockstars so happy that when recruiters call, they aren't interested. You want them to tell headhunters: "I love what I'm doing. I love the people I work with. We have a Rockstar team. We're delivering results. We're on a great mission, and I'm not going to risk that for a few more dollars." A 2017 study by Bamboo HR said the number one reason people leave their jobs is because of lack of career growth.

★ *Poor work/life balance.* Rockstars want the flexibility to integrate their life with their work. If you micromanage them and treat them like children, they'll seek greener pastures.

★ *Lousy manager.* People don't quit their job; they quit their manager. If you've recruited a Rockstar director of marketing but she's working under an average VP of marketing, your new hire is at risk from day one. She's going to get frustrated, be uninspired, and ultimately disconnected from the organization. Studies show that one's relationship with their manager accounts for half of job satisfaction. So, remove the lousy managers—now.

★ *Weak, ill-defined, or hostile culture.* This happens when you fail to hire on the basis of DNA match. So, make it non-negotiable in the recruiting process.

As the leader, your primary job is to remove these obstacles to high-performance. If you can do that, you won't lose many people. Guaranteed.

HOW TO KEEP YOUR ROCKSTARS

You've promised them a place where they can do their best work, so provide it. Create an environment where they'll flourish. This means the culture must be consistent. It means you only hire people who share your company DNA and you let go of people who don't. As you read that, you likely think, "Well, of course" but be honest; think about your team, about the two or three mis-hires or poor fits you've been dragging for months, if not years. What is holding you back from removing them?

"Environment" refers to the physical space, but it also refers to the boundaries. Rockstars need to know the parameters, and then need the flexibility to maneuver to deliver results within those parameters. They like to understand the end goal, the timeframe, the budget, and the boundaries and then be given some degree of freedom to design their own path to get there. It may not be the exact path you would have taken, but that's okay. You'll have created a far more loyal, engaged employee in the process.

Simple technology tools exist to help you check the pulse of your organization. I highly recommend TINYpulse, but there are others. These are fast, short, anonymous, employee-satisfaction surveys. Often, it's just one question. Using it with your staff weekly or monthly will reveal the trend line of engagement and morale. You may not always like the results, but just as dieters can't lose pounds without regular weigh-ins on a scale, it's vital to see how your team is feeling.

HOW TO COPE WHEN A ROCKSTAR LEAVES

Losing a Rockstar is an absolute crime. I've cried myself to sleep on more than one occasion. So, it's important to at least learn something from the loss. Do an exit interview (do it yourself; don't delegate it to HR). You're not trying to change the employee's mind, but you want to understand *why* they are leaving. I ask: "What could I have done differently? When did you know? When did the problem start? And how do I not repeat it with others?"

It could be, of course, that they were offered a role that simply doesn't exist at your company, or that they were offered a post overseas. You can do little to prevent those situations. But if they say, "Well, you began micromanaging me two months ago. We've talked about it, and I can't stand it anymore," it's vital to learn. Or else other Rockstars will follow.

Losing a Rockstar is demoralizing to the rest of your team

as well. It's another downside of hiring a Rockstar, in fact. When a Rockstar chooses to leave, it sends a message to the rest of the company that all is not well. They'll make their own guesses as to why the person left, and if they see the loss as part of a pattern, you've got work to do.

Regardless of others' assumptions, be sure to never disparage the person who has decided to leave. If you do, those who remain will worry that you'll do the same to them when they leave. They will also know you're not trustworthy because the person gave a Rockstar performance, yet you're disparaging them when they're absent. It is okay to express disappointment and even take some of the blame. It's okay to say, "I'm working on my leadership style so this doesn't happen again," or "I don't blame her. She had an amazing opportunity, and we couldn't compete with it as much as we tried."

If you've done your job by reading this book and building a consistent culture of Rockstars, then 20 percent of the time, the Rockstar who left will realize the grass wasn't greener after all.

So, treat your Rockstar well, even when they decide to leave your company. Wish them every success. Remind them what contributions they made and how impactful they were. Tell them that if the new opportunity isn't what they'd hoped, you'd love to talk to them about the possibility of coming back.

Reach out to them in two weeks, four weeks, six weeks. They may say, "I've made a mistake. I'd like to talk about returning." If that happens, welcome them back with open arms. That will increase your employee loyalty and reduce your attrition. A boomerang Rockstar is the best thing you could wish for. There's no better win. And no better signal to your team that the grass isn't always greener.

THE ALL-IMPORTANT FIVE CS

After hiring a Rockstar, the real work begins—getting the most out of them. I've studied and tried countless leadership styles. I'm convinced that authenticity wins—be yourself. But ensure that you provide what I call the five Cs to your Rockstars. They value these more than treadmills, ping pong tables, and notoriety.

CHALLENGE

First and foremost, provide them with interesting work. Give them customer problems to solve and a variety of people to deal with. Ask them to figure out how to make things faster, cheaper, and better within the organization. Countless studies show that challenge is the most important factor to job satisfaction for Rockstars, ranking even higher than money.

CAREER PATH

Rockstars are not only interested in their current role, but in their *next* one. They want to understand their likely career advancement and progression. That doesn't necessarily mean an annual promotion. It can include lateral moves to broaden skill sets or working in a different geography. You can also say, "Here are some potential options for what might come next. I can't promise them to you today, but if you do an outstanding job in this role, in a year, here are the kinds of things we see someone like you doing."

The average new hire will work with at least fifteen companies during their career. The average tenure at a company is two years. So, if you can keep a Rockstar aboard your "train" for longer than that, you're doing well. Go ahead and tell them, "My hope is to make this the best job of your life. If I do that, you'll likely stay with us for a sustained amount of time. My expectations are high, but they're realistic. My job is to get the best from you and provide the most fulfilling job you've ever had."

There's no need to have the career discussion more than every six months, but you need to understand their aspirations and how they evolve over time. That way, you can begin to think about their advancement and what other roles might make sense for them. Provide it before some headhunter does.

Part of career progression entails succession planning, so

that when you experience a departure, you have a potential successor identified. The best companies in the world often have a successor in mind for every role; that way, if someone leaves, they have a replacement named by the end of the day. The injury-riddled occupation of football has addressed this issue with the motto, "Next man up." Be prepared because you never know when a role will need to be refilled.

Bear in mind this will sometimes mean promoting a Rockstar who's not quite ready for the next step—you can do so on an interim basis. This is often better than taking the chance with an outside recruit, who would come with risk and could be the reason your Rockstar departs when passed over for the role. Always search inside first; at the very least, when considering outside candidates, run all viable internal candidates in parallel through the same fair and objective process.

CANDID COACHING

Most Rockstars respond well to candor, because they have an insatiable need to improve their performance. They recognize the path to promotion, to taking your job, and the CEO role perhaps one day, is to continually improve. To get better, they need and crave your feedback. So, provide it frequently. Ban the annual review; your Rockstars hate it as much as you detest cramming to write those missives over Christmas week. Instead, implement a monthly or quarterly coaching cycle. Find just two or three messages—not the laundry list given by most managers—that you want to reinforce, give specific examples, and then watch for improvement. When you catch them doing something right, reinforce it by letting them know you noticed and by recognizing them publicly if possible. Your two or three things should be tied to the skills they need for their next career move.

A powerful yet underused tool to help you give candid feedback is the Socratic method. Ask a few simple questions. "How do you think the (meeting/product launch/etc.) went? What could you have done differently? What could have gone better?" Rockstars are often their own toughest critic. Often, they are aware of what could have gone better or what they could have done differently. You can say, "What can I, as your manager, do next time to make sure your performance is better?"

Rockstars appreciate a work environment where candor, or a debate-and-align structure, is valued. This structure supports productive disagreements focused on the idea, not the person. Once a decision is reached, regardless of whether the group agreed or the leader reached a decision, everyone agrees to align behind that decision.

CONTACTS

Open your personal network—including your LinkedIn network—to your team. Introduce them to mentors outside the organization. This is especially important if yours is a small company where there just aren't many people for them to learn from. You might know people who would be great role models for your Rockstars. Some managers won't do this because they want to keep their Rockstar a secret, but when you introduce them to people who can broaden their knowledge, they will be grateful. And that increases loyalty.

COMPENSATION

Compensation isn't everything, but it's something. I've found that more important than the fixed base salary, however, is the variable upside. Rockstars respond well to a challenge, and they respond well to currency tied to upside performance. Lay out specifically how they earn it. Be clear with what percentage they can earn and when it will be paid out. And don't change the rules halfway through the game.

Rockstars don't respond well to black-box, or subjective, variable compensation. No matter how well they do, they don't know what they'll earn. That's not motivating, and so you're wasting your money and frustrating your top performers. Avoid capping your variable compensation. If they can deliver three times what you expect them to deliver, they should receive a meaningful variable compensation payout.

Perhaps my greatest frustration with regard to compensation is that so many leaders apply the "peanut butter" approach. They spread money around, approximately the same to all employees, in an effort to keep the peace. Instead, use differentiation, the concept of not treating everyone equally, to separate Rockstars from B- and C-Players. It means promotions, titles, and public recognition for great performances. It means fair compensation tied to performance. So rather than giving everyone 2 to 5 percent raises, give 20 percent raises to the ones who deserve it. And yes, that means you'll fund it by giving no raise this year to many. And those C-Players may choose to leave because of it. And that's okay.

Differentiation is the hallmark of a leader who is serious about keeping her Rockstars.

HOW TO HELP THEM IMPROVE

As the leader, it's your responsibility to teach your employees three sets of skills—through formal training and informal coaching. This will prepare Rockstars for their successive roles in the future:

1. *Functional job skills.* Be sure your employee knows how to do their job, the way your company expects it to be done. Don't presume that industry knowledge eliminates the need for training on specific job skills.
2. *Interpersonal skills.* It's not enough to know how to do their job. They also need to know how to deal with people; how

to debate, disagree, lead, inspire, coach, and—of course—recruit. Pass along your copy of this book once you finish. These vital skills aren't taught during formal education.

3. *Organizational skills.* Every company has its own policies; it's important that your employee knows how things are done within the organization; how decisions are made, and how individual compromise for the whole of the company leads to advancement.

Always be available when they need guidance, support, or help. Serve as a constant resource to them. Run interference for them—if you can't remove obstacles from their path, you're not a particularly useful manager for them. They need you to show them how to solve problems, not do it for them. Be sure, meanwhile, to connect what they do to the larger mission of the organization. Rockstars want to know why they are doing something or why a project is important.

Like anyone else, Rockstars need time, attention, and feedback. So, resist the temptation, particularly during their onboarding period, of being too hands-off; that's a common mistake for leaders of Rockstars.

In this chapter, we talked about what it takes to keep Rockstars, what happens when you lose a Rockstar, and ways to ensure high levels of performance.

CONCLUSION

CREATING YOUR OWN
ROCKSTARDOM

||||||||||||||||||

It's time. You've read the book and it's time to decide if you're ready to do the work. You now know how it's done. There are no secrets. I've held nothing back. It's simple, but it's not easy.

Do you want to commit to enjoying a Rockstar team at your company? Nothing says you must, and it's a lot of work. But as I've described, you're doing the work anyway today—motivating and micromanaging B-Players. Firing C-Players. Wouldn't you far prefer to invest the time up front, hire nothing but Rockstars, and let them advance your business to new heights?

That said, you can't do it on your own. If you agree with this approach—but the rest of your organization's leadership doesn't—you may be in the wrong place. With this approach, the organization must be all-in. This isn't the kind of thing that works well in isolation or in only one department.

Committing to put a Rockstar in every single seat in your organization is a gamechanger. It's been my number one priority in the companies that I've started and led. I persuade each of my clients to make it their number one priority, too. I implore you to do the same. But be all-in. Be totally committed to recruiting Rockstars, or don't waste your time.

Nothing will accelerate the growth of your company faster than a commitment to placing Rockstars in every role at every level. Launching a new product, improving your marketing, and streamlining operations are all great for business. But imagine if you had a multiple of improvement, as a result of exiting your low performers, creating a more consistent DNA, and attracting a steady stream of Rockstars. Nothing in business is more transformative.

You'll need to do less recruiting once your company is filled with Rockstars. If you're doing your job, you'll have less attrition because your Rockstars will want to stay. That creates more time for you to spend on other things.

And if you think all this is too expensive, I encourage you to look at how much money you're spending today on recruiting and mismanaging. Include the cost of executive recruiters, job postings, the staff time you spend interviewing poorly, the time you spend wining and dining candidates who don't join your company, the time you'll spend starting your search again when your top candidate says no, the missed opportunity when a sales territory is vacant for six months or the delay in shipping that new product because a key software developer role is vacant. You can afford to pay your Rockstars more if you get rid of these soft costs.

In a world that's moving ever faster, speed is everything. Capitalize on your opportunities by building a steady pipeline of talent. This will allow you to succession plan and fill seats in days and weeks, not months and quarters.

I've learned to see it as a cycle. We create a place where Rockstars thrive, so they come, they stay, the culture is powerful, and the business grows. As the business expands, we have more money, which we can use for differentiated compensation, and new opportunities for the Rockstars on our team. If a company is growing, it creates new career opportunities for its people by default. It's self-reinforcing.

And I've saved the best part for last. Your job becomes far easier. Imagine that your company is finally beating its forecasts, has a consistent culture, and low employee turnover. Your Board of Directors won't be on your case. You'll sleep better at night. You'll have less stress. You'll be able to take a vacation without worrying about the building blowing up while you're gone. This single most important skill in business will allow you to spend more time on the fun part of the business, which is creating, innovating, looking forward, and working with your Rockstars to make the concepts a reality.

The serendipity of this system is that, ultimately, you, as a leader, become a Rockstar as well. It comes full circle. In fact, if you crave a successful career, you must master the discipline of recruiting. And when you do, you'll make yourself invaluable to any business. As a leader, your job is to foster an environment where people can do their best work, give them the constraints and the room to run, develop them, and invest in them. The rest takes care of itself.

Everyone is looking for Rockstars. When you show your ability to field a team of them—thus, demonstrating your own Rockstar status—you, too, will be sought out by Boards of Directors, CEO's, and executive recruiters. You open up your career possibilities for advancement, making a name for yourself, as well as your company. The general manager who assembles a World Series champion is every bit the Rockstar that his athletes are and can then write his own ticket. Maybe *your* phone will start to ring off the hook. After all, headhunters know a Rockstar when they see one.

WHERE WE GO FROM HERE

||||||||||||||||||||

Our relationship need not end here.

I hope you'll join me on this journey and let me know how it's going. I want to be a resource for you. So, I've created a huge downloadable bonus package of materials. You can download it at RecruitRockstars.com/Bonus

And if you ever get stuck, visit my website RecruitRockstars.com, listen to my podcast, or just email me: Jeff@RecruitRockstars.com

Finally, I'd like to ask a small favor...

To help share my mission of "No Bad Hires," I'd be most grateful if you could write a short review of this book on Amazon. It takes just three minutes and is the best way to get the word out. Simply search for "Recruit Rockstars" in the Amazon search bar, select this book, scroll down to "Customer Reviews" and click the "Write a customer review" button.

You rock!

ABOUT THE
AUTHOR

||||||||||||||||||

JEFF HYMAN launched his recruiting career at Heidrick & Struggles and Spencer Stuart, the preeminent global executive search firms. Today, he's Chief Talent Officer at Chicago-based Strong Suit Executive Search. Along the way, Jeff created four companies, backed by $50 million in venture capital. He currently teaches the MBA course about recruiting at Northwestern University's Kellogg School of Management and hosts the five-star *Strong Suit Podcast*. Jeff has been featured by *Inc.*, *Fortune*, *Forbes*, *The Wall Street Journal*, CNBC, Bloomberg, and other media outlets. He holds a master's degree from Kellogg School of Management and a bachelor's degree from The Wharton School.